badajoz 1812

wellington's bloodiest siege

IAN FLETCHER

badajoz 1812

wellington's bloodiest siege

Praeger Illustrated Military History Series

Westport, Connecticut
London

Library of Congress Cataloging-in-Publication Data

Fletcher, Ian, 1957-
    Badajoz, 1812: Wellington's bloodiest siege / Ian Fletcher.
       p. cm. – (Praeger illustrated military history, ISSN 1547-206X)
    Originally published: Oxford: Osprey, 1999.
    Includes bibliographical references and index.
    ISBN 0-275-98617-9 (alk paper)
    1. Badajoz (Spain) – History – Siege, 18122. Peninsular War,   1807 -1814 –
    Campaigns – Spain. 3. Wellington, Arthur Wellesley, Duke of, 1769-1852 –
    Military leadership. I. Title. II. Series
    DC233.B26F55   2005
    940.2'742'094627 – dc22   2004061737

British Library Cataloguing in Publication Data is available.

First published in paperback in 1999 by Osprey Publishing Limited,
Midland House, West Way, Botley, Oxford OX2 0PH, UK
443 Park Avenue South, New York, NY 10016, USA
All rights reserved.

Library of Congress Catalog Card Number: 2004061737
ISBN: 0-275-98617-9
ISSN: 1547-206X

Praeger Publishers, 88 Post Road West, Westport, CT 06881
An imprint of Greenwood Publishing Group, Inc.
www.praeger.com

Printed in China through World Print Ltd.

The paper used in this book complies with the Permanent Paper Standard issued
by the National Information Standards Organization (Z39.48-1984).

10 9 8 7 6 5 4 3 2 1

CONTENTS

KEY TO MILITARY SYMBOLS

XXXXX ARMY GROUP	XXXX ARMY	XXX CORPS	XX DIVISION	X BRIGADE
III REGIMENT	II BATTALION	I COMPANY	INFANTRY	CAVALRY
ARTILLERY	ARMOUR	MOTORIZED	AIRBORNE	SPECIAL FORCES

INTRODUCTION

Napoleon once said that fortresses would not stop an army, but they would retard its progress. In the case of the mighty Spanish fortress of Badajoz he was absolutely correct. For not only did it prove to be a very sharp thorn in the side of the Allied army's progress in the Peninsula but it cost Wellington the flower of his army in the great assault that finally wrenched it from French hands on the night of 6 April 1812. The assault can hardly be described as successful, accompanied as it was by such great loss of life. Indeed, it was only the sheer determination of Wellington's men, driving themselves on through a maelstrom of fire against the town's massive walls, that won the day. The fall of Badajoz had terrible consequences for the town's population and the 72-hour period of debauchery, murder and destruction brought down upon it by the victorious soldiers of Wellington's army remains one of the most shameful episodes in the long history of the British army. The story of the siege and storming of Badajoz – and of its northern counterpart, Ciudad Rodrigo – is the subject of this book.

We need not dwell too long on the events which brought Britain's army to the Iberian Peninsula, nor on the course of the war up until the siege. These are amply covered in both the books on the Salamanca and Vittoria campaigns (Osprey Campaign Series numbers 48 and 59). Suffice to say that in the summer of 1808 Wellington, still Sir Arthur Wellesley at the time, had landed in Portugal with a small British army with which he very quickly defeated the French at both Roliça and Vimeiro to bring about an end to the first French invasion of Portugal and to the first phase of the war. After the ill-fated Corunna campaign of Sir John Moore in the winter of 1808-09, Wellesley returned to Portugal to thwart the second French invasion, at Oporto in May 1809. He was to remain in the Peninsula for a further five years before bringing the Peninsular War to a successful conclusion in April 1814. During that time he was to fight countless battles and sieges, march thousands of miles back and forth across the Peninsula, both in advance and in retreat, and defeat seven of Napoleon's much-vaunted Marshals; Victor, Ney, Kellerman, Marmont, Massena, Jourdan and Soult. He was also to win a plethora of titles from three grateful nations, Portugal, Spain and Britain. One of the titles was, of course, the name by which we know him today: Wellington.

The storming of Badajoz was probably the most awesome event of the entire Peninsular War. Indeed, such was the carnage at the breaches that, when he visited the scene on the morning of 7 April, Wellington wept openly at the sight of hundreds of his brave men, whose smoking, broken bodies lay piled up before the breaches following their unsuccessful attempts to break in, the decisive blows being struck elsewhere in the town. The next time he was to weep on the field of battle was on Sunday, 18 June 1815, following the battle of Waterloo.

OPERATIONS IN THE PENINSULA, 1811 – 1812

Marshal Bessiéres occupies northern Spain with 90,000 troops. He is relieved of command of the Army of the North in July 1811 and is replaced by Dorsenne

BESSIÉRES

The Army of Catalonia numbers 24,000 troops under the command of Marshal MacDonald, but these will not interfere with Allied plans in 1811

MACDONALD

On 10 May 1811, Brennier escapes with his garrison from Almeida. Thus, the last French foothold in Portugal is relinquished. Now, only the Spanish fortresses remain in French hands

Ciudad Rodrigo had been taken by Massena in July 1810. When Wellington besieged the town in January 1812, it was garrisoned by 1,937 under General Barrié

JOSEPH

The Army of Aragon numbers 51,000 troops under the command of Marshal Suchet. He is reinforced by 15,000 of Dorsenne's men in December 1811

At the end of 1811, Wellington's field army numbers around 46,000 troops. He survives largely because of the inability of the French to concentrate against him

MARMONT

Marmont commands the Army of Portugal numbering 58,000 troops. Joseph remains at Madrid with a further 25,000 men of the Army of the Centre

SUCHET

WELLINGTON

Badajoz falls to the French in March 1811. When Wellington approaches the place in March the following year, it is garrisoned by 5,000 men under the command of General Armand Phillipon, who had successfully defended the town in May and June 1811

16 May 1811: Beresford defeats Soult at Albuera and prevents the latter from relieving the town

Over 350,000 French troops occupy Spain but these are tied down by the presence of both the Spanish guerrillas and the regular Spanish armies and are unable to concentrate to act against Wellington

May–June 1811, Wellington and Beresford lay siege to Badajoz, but the attacks directed against Fort San Christobal fail disastrously

In September 1811, Marmont and the Army of Portugal joins forces with Dorsenne who, having left the larger part of the Army of the North to garrison northern Spain, marches south to link up with Marmont. This gives the French a combined total of almost 60,000 men against which Wellington could only muster 46,000. However, in December 1811, Marmont is ordered by Napoleon to detach 15,000 troops to assist Suchet at Valencia, thus weakening his force and giving Wellington the opportunity to move against Ciudad Rodrigo

By the end of 1811, thousands of French troops have been withdrawn from Spain to take part in Napoleon's ill-fated Russian campaign the following year

SOULT

Soult's Army of the South numbers 90,000 troops. His field army, however, numbers just 25,000 as the remainder are required to garrison Seville, Grenada, Cordoba and Jaen

| 0 | | 100 Miles |
| 0 | | 200 Km |

CHRONOLOGY

1807

| 18 October | French troops cross the Spanish frontier. |
| 30 November | Junot occupies Lisbon. |

1808

23 March	The French occupy Madrid.
2 May	Uprising in Madrid, the 'Dos de Mayo'.
14 July	The French, under Bessiéres, defeat the Spaniards, under Cuesta and Blake, at Medina del Rio Seco.
22 July	The French, under Dupont, surrender at Baylen.
1 August	A British force, under Sir Arthur Wellesley, lands at Mondego Bay, Portugal.
17 August	Wellesley defeats Delaborde at Roliça.
21 August	Wellesley defeats Junot at Vimeiro.
30 August	Convention of Cintra: Wellesley recalled to England.

30 October	The French evacuate Portugal.
8 November	Napoleon enters Spain with 80,000 men.
4 December	Napoleon occupies Madrid.
December	Sir John Moore advances from Salamanca.
21 December	Lord Paget's cavalry defeats the French at Sahagun.
29 December	Paget gives a repeat performance at Benavente.

1809

January	Retreat to Corunna.
16 January	Moore killed at the battle of Corunna.
22 April	Wellesley returns to Portugal.
12 May	Wellesley crosses the Douro and defeats Soult at Oporto.
28-29 July	Wellesley defeats the French at Talavera.
4 September	Wellesley is created Viscount Wellington of Talavera.

1810

10 July	Massena takes Ciudad Rodrigo.
24 July	Craufurd defeated by Ney on the Coa River.
27 September	Wellington victorious over Massena at Busaco.
10 October	Wellington enters the Lines of Torres Vedras.
14 October	Massena discovers Lines and halts.
17 November	Massena withdraws to Santarem.

1811

5 March	Sir Thomas Graham victorious at Barrosa.
10 March	Soult takes Badajoz.
3-5 May	Wellington defeats Massena at Fuentes de Oñoro.
6 May	Beresford begins first British siege of Badajoz.
11 May	Brennier abandons Almeida to Wellington.
16 May	Beresford defeats Soult at Albuera.
19 May -17 June	Second British siege of Badajoz. It ends in bloody failure.

The French sortie at Ciudad Rodrigo on 14 January 1812. Working parties, in their shirt sleeves, get to grips with French troops who are attempting to fill in the trenches and damage the works.

1812

8 January	Siege of Ciudad Rodrigo begins.
19 January	Wellington takes Ciudad Rodrigo by storm.
February-March	Wellington's army moves south to lay siege to Badajoz for a third time.
16 March	Third siege of Badajoz begins.
6 April	Badajoz is assaulted by Wellington's infantry. The fortress falls shortly after midnight.
7-9 April	Badajoz is sacked mercilessly by Wellington's victorious infantry.
22 July	Wellington defeats Marmont at Salamanca.
12 August	Wellington enters Madrid.
19 September	Wellington begins siege of Burgos.
22 October	Wellington abandons siege of Burgos.
22 Oct. -19 Nov.	Allied retreat to Portugal.
19 November	Allied army arrives at Ciudad Rodrigo.

1813

21 June	Wellington defeats Joseph at Vittoria, created Field Marshal.
25 July	Soult makes counterattack in the Pyrenees. Battles at Maya and Roncesvalles.
28-30 July	Wellington defeats Soult at Sorauren.
31 August	Graham takes San Sebastian by storm.
31 August	Soult repulsed at San Marcial.
7 October	Wellington crosses the Bidassoa into France.
25 October	Pamplona surrenders.
10 November	Wellington defeats Soult at the Battle of the Nivelle.
9-12 December	Wellington defeats Soult at the Battle of the Nive.
13 December	Soult repulsed by Hill at St Pierre.

1814

27 February	Wellington defeats Soult at Orthes.
6 April	Napoleon abdicates.
10 April	Wellington defeats Soult at Toulouse.
14 April	French sortie from Bayonne.
17 April	Soult surrenders.
27 April	Bayonne surrenders.
30 April	Treaty of Paris.
3 May	Wellington created Duke.

A view of Ciudad Rodrigo from the north, taken from the site of the first parallel on the Greater Teson. From here it is easy to see why the occupation of the Greater Teson was so vital to any besieging force, overlooking the walls of the town as it did. The Lesser Teson lies beneath the flats in the centre of this photo. To see how the town has changed in the last 30 years, this photo should be compared with Plate 27 in Jac Weller's *Wellington in the Peninsula*.

OPPOSING PLANS

The importance of Badajoz lay in the fact that it commanded the southern corridor between Spain and Portugal, the fortress of Elvas was its counterpart on the Portuguese side of the border. Elvas itself was not a particularly strong place. It had been occupied by the French during General Junot's invasion back in 1807 but they had been forced to relinquish it under the terms of the Convention of Cintra the following year and it remained in Allied hands throughout the remainder of the war. The northern corridor between the two countries was commanded by Ciudad Rodrigo on the Spanish side and Almeida on the Portuguese. Any army wishing to move freely between the two countries would need to take these fortresses as it would be most unwise to leave them occupied in its rear, free to hinder communications. They were the two natural and traditional invasion routes into Portugal, the country between Badajoz and Ciudad Rodrigo was mountainous and virtually impassable. In October 1807, Junot had passed through this barren and mountainous region in order to enter Portugal, the event which ostensibly sparked off the war, but he did it at a tremendous cost to his army. Indeed, the shattered, exhausted state of his army bore testament to the folly of considering it as an invasion route when it arrived piecemeal in Lisbon in November 1807. No, he who controlled the fortress towns of Ciudad Rodrigo and Badajoz controlled the two great invasion routes. They were, in effect, the 'keys of Spain'.

When Wellington's army arrived before the walls of Badajoz in March 1812 it did so with two failed attempts behind it. The two previous sieges

This is what a Napoleonic breach really looks like. This is just one of the breaches at Fort Conception, a few miles north of Fuentes de Oñoro. The fort was blown up by Wellington's engineers on 21 July 1810 as his army pulled back into Portugal following the capture by Massena of Ciudad Rodrigo. Note how the debris from the explosion has created a sort of ramp. Such a ramp was created by Wellington's gunners at both Ciudad Rodrigo and Badajoz in order to facilitate the stormers' ascent into the breaches.

A view from the site of the Great Breach at Ciudad Rodrigo looking out towards the Greater and Lesser Tesons. The Greater Teson forms the horizon, while the open space to the left of the flats is where the northern end of the second parallel was situated on the Lesser Teson. In fact, battery no. 5 would have been sited immediately behind the flats.

of Badajoz, in May and June 1811, had resulted in bloody failure and it was this, and the desire to 'settle the score', which was to prove one of the causes for the shocking events which followed the storming on 6 April. The town had fallen to Marshal Soult in March 1811 after a very fine protracted defence by the Spanish governor, Menacho. Unfortunately, he was killed and his successor, Imaz, possessing none of Menacho's attributes, treacherously surrendered the town to Soult on 10 March, thus sparing the French the ordeal of an assault and the town of a potential sacking. This came as a blow to the Allied war effort as Wellington had only just begun to drive Massena and his starving army from Portugal after the latter's futile sojourn before the Lines of Torres Vedras. Massena was finally driven from Portugal on 3 April 1811, whereupon Wellington could turn his mind to besieging Ciudad Rodrigo. The news, therefore, that Badajoz had fallen to the French came as a setback to him.

Undeterred, Wellington decided that both Badajoz and Ciudad Rodrigo must be taken before he could consider any move into Spain. His strategy involved dividing his army and while he himself remained in the north blockading the fortress of Almeida – which the French abandoned on 11 May – William Carr Beresford marched south to lay siege to Badajoz. The first siege was raised on 13 May 1811 when Beresford marched to meet Soult, approaching from the south, at Albuera. The resulting battle there on 16 May was one of the bloodiest of the war, the sheer staying power of the British infantry providing Beresford with the key to his victory. But it was a victory won at a great cost, with some 6,000 Allied casualties, 4,000 of which were British, and it was a tired and very bruised Allied army which renewed the siege of Badajoz the following month.

The second siege, in June 1811, was a complete failure. It was directed mainly against the fort on the north bank of the river Guadiana, Fort San Christobal. The attempts against the fort were made by escalade, that is by means of ladders placed in the ditches, up which Beresford's stormers would have to climb, all the time under fire from the defenders. The ensuing assaults were met with great ferocity by the defenders, many of whom simply rolled grenades and barrels of gunpowder over the ramparts to explode amongst the stormers in the

The ruins of the convent of San Francisco in the suburbs of Ciudad Rodrigo. It was here that the Light Division assembled to begin its assault on the Lesser Breach on the night of 19 January 1812.

confined spaces of the ditches below. It is hardly surprising, therefore, that these unimaginative attacks were repulsed with heavy loss. The siege was raised once again on 17 June and the army slipped away to the north leaving Badajoz in the hands of a justifiably triumphant French garrison.

The remainder of 1811 was spent largely in a series of manoeuvres on the Portuguese-Spanish border as Marmont – now in command after Massena's recall to France – and Wellington each sought to gain some advantage. None was gained by either and the year petered out with Ciudad Rodrigo and Badajoz still in French hands. There were, however, some significant developments in the Peninsula as a result of Napoleon's planned invasion of Russia. Thousands of good French troops were recalled to be replaced by conscripts and troops of a lesser calibre, a move which certainly weakened the French forces in Spain. This may not appear to have been too serious for the French, however, as they could still muster around 350,000 troops to oppose Wellington. Fortunately for the Allied commander, they were unable to do so as a result of a combination of internal bickering between the various French commanders in Spain and as a result of the almost tireless efforts by both the Spanish armies and the guerrillas, who tied down thousands of French troops who might otherwise have been free to concentrate against Wellington. Their part in the war should never be overlooked. A critical example of this was the withdrawal of several thousand French troops from the Ciudad Rodrigo area, who were ordered to march east to assist in the struggle against the Spanish forces there. This suddenly gave Wellington a window of opportunity to be able to act against Ciudad Rodrigo without the threat of a strong French force interfering with him.

The decision to withdraw these troops was a critical one and Wellington was quick to seize the initiative. He had already formulated his plans for the investment of Ciudad Rodrigo but was unsure as to the timing of his attack. All we know is that he was prepared to move should the opportunity arise. Furthermore, we know that he had decided to move south against Badajoz in the February or March of 1812 whether Ciudad Rodrigo had fallen or not. His army had already been busy making gabions and fascines and other siege impedimenta. Supplies, guns and ammunition had been gathered and brought forward and plans made for the siege of the town. Then, upon receipt of the information of the withdrawal east of some 12,000 French troops, Wellington moved forward, a bold move that went against all conventions of the day, it being winter, and a very bad winter at that, a time when armies stopped campaigning and went into cantonments. Meanwhile, General Barrié, governor of Ciudad Rodrigo, settled down for the winter, safe in the knowledge that little would be done to interfere with him until the spring when the campaigning season began once again. Little did he know that his winter sojourn was about to come to an abrupt and violent end.

OPPOSING COMMANDERS

RIGHT **Sir Arthur Wellesley, 1st Duke of Wellington (1769-1852). After a painting by Heaphy, depicting him at the siege of San Sebastian. Wellington commanded the Anglo-Portuguese army in the Peninsula between 1808 and 1814 and, save for a period of six months following the Convention of Cintra in August 1808, did so without a single day's leave.**

Sir Thomas Picton (1758-1815). Picton himself was one of the great firebrands in Wellington's army. He was as brave as a lion and had served in the Peninsula since 1810.

French Commanders

The French garrison was commanded by General Armand Phillipon, a very experienced soldier who had enlisted in the Bourbon army in 1778 and who, by 1790, had risen to the rank of sergeant-major. During the following years he saw active service in Italy, Switzerland and Hanover, had served with the Grand Armée from 1805 to 1807 and had fought at Austerlitz. He was transferred to Spain in 1808 and fought at Talavera and at the siege of Cadiz. He was made a baron in 1810 and promoted to general de brigade. He was appointed governor of Badajoz in March 1811 and repulsed the Allied attacks later that year. In July 1811 he was promoted to general de division. Sadly, there appear to be no paintings of this very brave and very competent soldier. He was ably supported in his job by his chief engineer, Colonel Lamarc, to whom we are indebted for the French version of the siege of Badajoz and whose defensive works would be the cause of so many deaths in Wellington's army.

Marshal Nicolas Soult, Duke of Dalmatia (1769-1851). Soult's greatest attributes were his logistical and organisational skills and, in particular, his ability to get his men to the battlefield. However, as Wellington himself was once to remark, he did not know what to do with them once he had got them there. In May 1811 he was defeated by Beresford at Albuera when marching to relieve Badajoz. The following year he represented Phillipon's greatest chance of relief but, as in 1811, he failed.

Marshal Auguste Marmont, Duke of Ragusa (1774-1852). Marmont commanded the Army of Portugal during the sieges of both Ciudad Rodrigo and Badajoz in 1812. Having lost his siege train to Wellington when the latter took Ciudad Rodrigo, he was in no position to threaten the town when Wellington marched south to besiege Badajoz. However, he could probably have done more to intervene during the siege there in March and April 1812.

The Allies

Sir Arthur Wellesley, 1st Duke of Wellington (1769-1852). The sieges in the Peninsula were not Wellington's finest achievements, the operations being mere bludgeon work. Faced with a lack of decent tools and no corps of sappers and miners, Wellington relied on the brawn of his superb infantry to take first Ciudad Rodrigo, then Badajoz and, finally,

Sir Richard Fletcher (1768-1813). Wellington's chief engineer was badly wounded at the siege of Badajoz but continued to work from his tent and was consulted by Wellington each day. He was killed during the assault on San Sebastian on 31 August 1813.

Marshal Auguste Marmont, Duke of Ragusa (1774-1852). A veteran fighter of several campaigns and ADC to Napoleon in 1796, he was appointed to command in Spain on 7 May 1811, replacing Marshal Massena.

Marshal Nicolas Soult, Duke of Dalmatia (1769-1851). The first Marshal of France, Soult was called the ablest tactician in Europe by Napoleon after his decisive role in the battle of Austerlitz. From 1808 he served in Spain, driving Sir John Moore back to Corunna though he was unable to defeat him decisively.

William Carr Beresford (1764-1854). Beresford was one of Wellington's most trusted subordinates who nevertheless blotted his copybook by his handling of the army at Albuera on 16 May 1811.

San Sebastian. They only failed to take Burgos when, by Wellington's own admission, he overreached himself, undertaking the siege with just three heavy guns.

Sir Thomas Picton (1758-1815). Commanded the 'Fighting' 3rd Division at both Ciudad Rodrigo and Badajoz and was wounded leading his men into action at the latter place. Supremely brave, Picton was seen in Ciudad Rodrigo after the fall of the town, beating drunken soldiers with a broken musket and damning everybody within earshot. He died a hero's death at Waterloo in 1815.

Sir Richard Fletcher (1768-1813). Wellington's chief engineer and the man behind the construction of the Lines of Torres Vedras. Fletcher was badly wounded at the siege of Badajoz but continued to work from his tent and was consulted by Wellington each day. Like his fellow officers of the Royal Engineers, Fletcher did not shirk his duties in the front line and was killed during the assault on San Sebastian on 31 August 1813.

William Carr Beresford (1764-1854). Beresford is best remembered for his organisational skills and, in particular, with the organisation of the Portugese army. In spite of his bungling of the battle of Albuera on 16 May 1811, Beresford was Wellington's own choice to suceed him in the event of anything happening to himself. Beresford supervised the first two sieges of Badajoz in May and June 1811, both of which ended in failure.

OPPOSING ARMIES

French Forces

The garrison at Badajoz consisted of 4,500 men, although some 400 of these were sick in hospital. Given the extent of the town and its outworks this number was considered by Phillippon to be too few to ensure a really strong defence and he would have to call upon all his powers of leadership to ensure his men were in the right place at the right time when the assault came. Indeed, the deployment of his men would need a great deal of consideration. Bastions 1 and 2 would be held by the 9th Léger, bastions 3 and 4 by the 28th Léger, bastion 5 by the 58th Regiment and bastions 6 and 7 by the 103rd Regiment. The defence of the castle and bastions 8 and 9 was entrusted to the German troops of the Hesse D'Armstadt. A detachment of Spanish troops in the service of King Joseph was detailed to hold the Las Palmas Gate, as were the men of the armed civil departments. The 88th Regiment and the small number of cavalry were placed in reserve in the Plaza de San Juan. A detachment of the 64th Regiment was attached to the artillery and the 50 sappers used as gunners.

A view of Ciudad Rodrigo from the western end of the Lesser Teson, close to the site of one of the forward saps. The 'terracing' visible in front of the cathedral marks the glacis in front of the Great Breach. The breaching battery no. 5 was situated about 250 yards to the left of this picture and now lies beneath a block of flats.

Phillipon also formed a special company of men from the best marksmen in each battalion who were to harass the workmen in the trenches. This company was organised by General Veiland and was commanded jointly by Lieutenant Michel of the 9th Léger and Leclerc de Ruffey of the 58th. Command of Fort Pardaleras was entrusted to Colonel Pineau, Colonel Gaspard Thierry was placed in command of Fort Picurina and Captain Villain in command of Fort San Christobal. The castle of Badajoz was put under the command of Colonel Knoller. The garrison may not have been strong numerically, but it was experienced, it had seen off Wellington the previous year, was high in morale and was relatively well supplied with provisions – a convoy of 60 mules laiden with flour had entered Badajoz just prior to the encirclement of the town. All augered well for a long, protracted and vigorous defence and there was no reason to doubt that enough time could be bought for either Marmont or Soult to come to their rescue. With its extremely forbidding walls Badajoz was a very strong fortress. It had defied Wellington's men in 1811 and would come very close to doing so again in 1812.

The French Garrison of Ciudad Rodrigo

34th Léger, one battalion	975
113th Ligne, one battalion	577
Artillery, 2 companies	168
Engineers	15
Non-combatants, (Civil officers, etc.)	36
Sick in hospital	163
Staff	3
Total	**1,937**

The French Garrison at Badajoz

Staff	25
3/39th Léger	580
1/28th Léger	597
1/58th Ligne	450
3/88th Ligne	600
3/103rd Ligne	540
64th Ligne (2 companies)	130
Hesse D'Armstadt (2 Battalions)	910
Cavalry	42
Artillery	261
Engineers and Sappers	260
Sick in hospital	300
Non-combatants (Civil officers, etc.)	254
Total	**5,003**

Allied Forces

The strategy and tactics employed by Wellington's army have been well covered by historians over the years and are well enough known. Indeed, ample coverage is given to Wellington's infantry in the two Osprey Men-at-Arms volumes 114 and 119. However, the siege of Badajoz was not about columns, lines or squares. Nor was it about the firepower of the British infantry line. No, during the sieges in the Peninsula it was Wellington's artillery and engineers who took centre stage throughout the initial stages, with the infantry coming on for the finale when flesh and blood took on fire and stone. Nevertheless, it is worth taking a look at the troops who were to carry out the business of digging the trenches and constructing the batteries, as well as delivering the actual assaults.

At Ciudad Rodrigo, all of the besieging divisions, the 1st, 3rd, 4th and Light, did shifts lasting 24 hours each, in the trenches, even the 'Gentlemen's Sons', the Foot Guards in the army's 1st Division. First to begin work was the Light Division, containing some of the finest regiments in the army, including the 43rd and 52nd Light Infantry regiments and the famous 95th Rifles. The Light Division were in the trenches from 8–9 January, the 12th to the 13th, the 16th to the 17th and for the actual storm on 19 January. The 1st Division did shifts on 9 to 10 January, the 13th to the 14th and the 17th to the 18th. The 3rd Division worked from the 11th to the 12th, the 15th to the 16th and, like the Light Division, were in the trenches on the evening of the assault. The 4th Division was in the trenches from 10 to 11 January, the 14th to the 15th and the 18th to the 19th.

The men themselves were not particularly experienced at siege warfare, Badajoz was the only fortress to have been besieged so far in the war; and even then it was only Fort San Christobal that really came under serious attack. However, the troops were more than qualified to make the actual attack upon Ciudad Rodrigo, the men of the 3rd and Light Divisions, in particular, were two of Wellington's finest divisions. Indeed, the 3rd Division, nicknamed the 'Fighting' division, contained some of the most fearsome fighters in the Allied army, none more so than the 88th (Connaught) Rangers. Craufurd's Light Division was no ordinary division

Robert Craufurd directs his Light Division to the Lesser Breach on the night of 19 January 1812. The men have left their packs in camp while others carry ladders. Craufurd was to be mortally wounded minutes later. After a painting by Wollen.

either, and the mere presence of the 95th Rifles in any formation was enough to make it very different. Although Ciudad Rodrigo boasted none of the terrible defences that so thwarted Wellington's assault upon Badajoz, the town still had to be taken, and it is a testament to the prowess of these two fine divisions that it fell in a relatively short space of time. Nevertheless, we should never forget the many other good, solid regiments that saw action, not only at the sieges, but elsewhere in the Peninsula, regiments that often go overlooked with the 95th Rifles in particular attracting much attention. Indeed, some regiments, such as the 28th (North Gloucestershire) Regiment, fought in almost every action of the war, including Albuera, a battle that not even the 95th can claim as a battle honour.

When the time came for Badajoz to be attacked the Light and 3rd Divisions were once again to the fore. On this occasion, however, part of the army, including the 1st Division, which had been present at Ciudad Rodrigo, marched south to cover the siege operations and were not, therefore, involved in the siege. When the time came for the assault to be delivered it was the 3rd and Light Divisions who were again in action, along with the 4th and 5th Divisions. Sadly, the Light and 4th were not able to break into the town, as we shall see, but Leith's 5th Division and Picton's 3rd were successful.

The regiments at both sieges were well below strength. On paper each battalion should have comprised ten companies, each of around 100 men, but by this stage of the Peninsular War the number of men had been so reduced, as a result either of battle or, more likely, sickness, that some weak battalions were later merged with each other to form Provisional Battalions. During the stormings it mattered little how strong each battalion was. As already stated, strategy and tactics were simply not

The ditch in front of the walls at Ciudad Rodrigo, close to the spot where the 94th Foot entered before turning to its left – i.e. towards the camera. From this angle it is possible to see how the two guns placed beneath the castle, visible to the right of this photo, enfiladed the ditches.

A wonderful view of Ciudad Rodrigo from the air. The site of the Great Breach was in the angle of the walls at the bottom left-hand corner of this photo. The site of the Lesser Breach, stormed by the Light Division, was at the location marked by the road that enters the town on the left. In 1812 a tower stood at this point, before Allied artillery brought it tumbling down into the ditch. The 94th attacked the Great Breach by first negotiating the fausse braie at the bottom centre before entering the ditch and turning to its left to attack the breach. The 5th entered the ditch just below the castle, right, before turning to its left to make for the breach. The importance of the task given to O'Toole – the silencing of the two guns placed in the castle enclosure which were to enfilade the attacking columns – can be appreciated from this photo. The river Agueda flows at top right.

applicable during a storming and it was simply a matter of throwing as many men as was possible at the breaches. It is difficult to imagine how commanders controlled their men in such circumstances and, indeed, this must have been very difficult, but we do know that many officers of some of the better battalions did manage to maintain order after the successful stormings, which says much for their own abilities and for the discipline of their men, particularly when we consider the disorders that followed each storming.

However, for all of their heroic efforts during the sieges, the infantry would never have been able to storm either of the towns had it not been for the vital preparatory work carried out by both the Royal Engineers and Royal Artillery.

In 1812, the Corps of Royal Engineers was a far different corps from that which we know today. Indeed, it was exclusively formed of officers, who wore a dark blue uniform which often caused confusion amongst Wellington's allies. Chief engineer was Sir Richard Fletcher, whose greatest and most famous achievement was the construction of the Lines of Torres Vedras. The idea behind these defensive lines to the north of Lisbon was not a new one but Fletcher was the man who turned the idea into reality. He commanded a very dedicated and highly trained band of fellow Royal Engineers but they were disgracefully too few in number. Indeed, in a damning comment in his great *History of the War in the Peninsula*, William Napier was moved to write, 'The sieges carried on by the British in Spain were a succession of butcheries, because the commonest materials and means necessary for their art were denied to the engineers'. And, of the siege of Badajoz in 1811, he wrote, 'The regular engineer officers were twenty-one in number; eleven volunteers from the line were joined as assistant engineers; and a draft of three hundred

intelligent infantry, including twenty-four artificers of the staff corps, strengthened the force immediately under their command. It is not strange that the siege failed. It was strange and culpable that the British Government should have sent an engineer corps into the field so ill-organised and equipped that all the officers' bravery and zeal could not render it efficient'. The shortage of Royal Engineers in the Peninsula was compounded by their high casualty rate as they were frequently required to guide the storming columns to their objectives. Sir Richard Fletcher himself would become a casualty at San Sebastian in 1813.

The Royal Engineers were backed up by the Royal Military Artificers, a small corps which had been set up in the late 18th century to replace the need for civilian workmen. These were also far too few in number. In February 1812, Wellington himself urged the government to create a corps of sappers and miners and a warrant was duly issued that same year, with the Royal Military Artificers becoming the Corps of Royal Military Artificers and Royal Sappers and Miners, which was thankfully shortened to simply the Corps of Royal Sappers and Miners, although by the time of the siege of San Sebastian in 1813 there were still too few of them. The siege of Badajoz in 1812, therefore, was waged with just a few Royal Engineers and it was the ordinary line infantry who bore the brunt of the work, digging the parallels and constructing the batteries. In all, it was not a satisfactory situation but it had to do.

If it was the job of the Royal Engineers to decide where the walls should be breached, it was the Royal Artillery to whom the task of

'The Storming of Ciudad Rodrigo'. This picture shows quite clearly how the ladders were placed in the ditches for ease of descent as opposed to ascent. The stormers then had the task of climbing the breach itself, which, as can be seen, forms a kind of ramp. A good, active garrison commander would try to clear away as much of the debris as possible to prevent such a 'ramp' being formed. On the whole, this Victorian picture is rather accurate, save for the uniforms. The walls, however, are strikingly similar to those at Ciudad Rodrigo.

The Light Division's view of the site of the Lesser Breach at Ciudad Rodrigo. The breach was made in the walls where the tunnel is now situated. In 1812 it was the site of a small tower, which was demolished by Wellington's gunners. This photograph was taken while standing on the fausse braie.

breaching the walls actually fell. Like their colleagues in the Royal Engineers, the officers of the Royal Artillery were professional men, trained in the art of gunnery, and much depended upon their skill to be able to make practicable breaches in the walls of the town, breaches that had to be made wide and clean, and made in the fastest possible time. Anyone who has seen the damage to the cathedral and the buildings behind the breaches at Ciudad Rodrigo, as a result of some very wayward firing, will find it hard to believe that the artillery fire in the Peninsula was little more than a hit-or-miss affair. It was far more scientific than that, however, and good officers would have studied Ayde's Pocket Bombadier and would very quickly have gauged both range and direction of their targets, which, from the distance from where their guns were positioned, would appear very small indeed. The huge 24- and 18-pounder guns would then set about pummelling the foot of the walls in order to bring the whole wall tumbling down to create a sort of ramp up which the stormers would be able to charge. Then it was down to the tenacity and determination of the stormers. Wellington's gunners had 52 heavy guns available to them during the siege, sixteen of which were 24-pounders, sixteen were 24-pound hotwitzers, and the remainder Russian 18-pounders. The 24-pounder guns, with their nine-foot-long barrels, were the guns which would do the most damage, backed up by the 18-pounders. On the face of it there would appear to be little to choose between them but Jones, in his *Journal of the Sieges,* quite clearly says that the effect produced by the 24-pounder is so much greater than that produced by an 18-pounder that no engineer should ever be satisfied with the latter when the possibility existed of being able to use 24-pounders. For these heavy guns alone there were 22,367 shells of round shot available to the gunners during the siege as well as 24,983 shells of other calibres. By the end of the siege, Wellington's gunners would have used a total of 2,253 barrels of powder and, with each barrel weighing 90lbs, it may well be imagined just how much work the artillery got through at Badajoz.

Wellington possessed no sappers or miners and the
business of digging paralells and batteries had to be done
by the ordinary line infantry who thoroughly hated the job.
The men would work in awful conditions with snow and ice
at Ciudad Rodrigo and freezing rain at Badajoz. There was
little shelter from enemy fire particularly at Badajoz where
the mud refused to pile up and simply ran back into the
trenches. A shortage of cutting tools made the job even
harder. This painting shows the men at work before the
walls of Badajoz amidst heavy rain. In the distance can be
seen the immensely strong walls whilst to the right, situated
high above the rest of the town, stands the castle, which
was attacked by the 3rd Division during the storming
on 6 April 1812.

RV. 99

ALLIED TROOPS AT THE STORMING OF CIUDAD RODRIGO

3rd Division

Mackinnon's Brigade	1/45th, 5/60th, 1/88th
Campbell's Brigade	2/5th, 77th, 2/83rd, 94th

Light Division

Vandeleur's Brigade	1/52nd, 2/52nd, 3/95th, 3rd Caçadores
Barnard's Brigade	1/43rd, 1/95th, 2/95th
Pack's Portuguese Brigade	1st, 16th Regiments
Power's Portuguese Brigade	9th, 21st Line Regiments

ALLIED TROOPS AT THE STORMING OF BADAJOZ

3rd Division

Kempt's Brigade	1/45th, 5/60th, 74th, 1/88th
Campbell's Brigade	2/5th, 77th, 2/83rd, 94th

4th Division

Kemmis's Brigade	3/27th, 1/40th
Bowe's Brigade	1/7th, 1/23rd, 1/48th

5th Division

Hay's Brigade	3/1st, 1/9th, 2/38th
Walker's Brigade	1/4th, 2/30th, 2/44th
Light Division	1/43rd, 1/52nd, 1/95th, 3/95th
Portuguese Regiments	3rd, 11th, 15th, 21st and 23rd Line
	1st, 3rd, 6th and 8th Caçadores

DETAIL OF THE PROPORTION OF TOOLS AND STORES ORDERED FOR THE SIEGE OF BADAJOZ, MARCH-APRIL 1812. (TAKEN FROM JONES' JOURNAL OF THE SIEGES.)

Shovels	1,000	Adzes, carpenters'	30
Chests of tools, carpenters	2	Chalk lines, with reels	10
Spare helves	150	Claw-hammers, large	30
Sand bags, bushel	80,000	Box rulers, 2-feet	20
Pick-axes	1,200	Do. small	30
Broad-axes	60	Oil stones	6
Spare helves	300	Gimlets, spike	40
Felling-axes	300	Wood squares	0
Spades	300	Do. common	20
Miners' tools for 20 miners		Do. levels	10
Mattocks	200	Spun yarn, coils	12
Levels with lines and bobs	6	Iron squares	5
Tarpaulins, large	20	Hambro'line, skeins	20
Smiths' tools for 10 smiths		Ballast baskets	100
Do. small	20	Hand hatchets,	300
Forge carts, complete	2	Hand-crow levers, 6-feet	10
Spikes, 7-inch	6,000	Do. bills	500
Steel, cwts.	2	Do. 5½ feet	10
Do. 10-inch	1,000	Sledge-hammers	20
Coals, chaldron	1	Tents, complete, for officers	10
Saws, hand	30	Tallow, firkins	2
Nails, of sizes	20,000	Do. for men	10
Do. pit	12	Grease, kegs	6
Planes, of sorts	6	Fascine chokers	12
Do. cross cut	6	Chalk, a small quantity	
Gouges	20	Do. mallets	40
Setters, and files for Augers,		Scaling ladders, joints	36
of sizes the above, a good proportion	20	Dark lanthorns	12
Compasses, pairs	20	White rope coils, 2½ inch	2

RIGHT **British troops storming a fortress by escalade in the Peninsula. This illustration by Harry Payne purports to show the attack on Ciudad Rodrigo, although it is more likely that it depicts events at the castle at Badajoz. Some of the details are correct, such as the men having left their knapsacks in camp, although the artist has the men wearing the 1812-pattern shako, which had yet to reach the Peninsula.**

SIEGE WARFARE

'One day's trench-work,' wrote John Kincaid of the 95th Rifles, 'is as like another as the days themselves; and like nothing better than serving an apprenticeship to the double calling of grave-digger and game-keeper, for we found ample employment for both the spade and the rifle'. From this it may be gathered that Wellington's men did not take too kindly to siege work. In fact, they positively loathed it. Unlike the French army, Wellington possessed no corps of sappers and miners and the digging of trenches, or parallels as they were called, fell to the infantry of the line. This, of course, was not why they joined the army. If they had wanted to spend their days digging holes they might as well have joined a gang of navvies working on roads and canals. The work was dangerous and despised by them but it had to be done, hence the great dislike of siege work.

The actual business of a siege was relatively straightforward in terms of an overall operation, but the various elements that comprised the whole were often quite complex, such as identifying the points of attack, the tracing out of the ground, the digging of the parallels and saps and the siting and construction of gun batteries. It was here that the small band of Royal Engineers really came into their own. Sadly, there were simply too few of them and even this small band of brothers was slowly and steadily reduced in numbers following casualties in the various sieges. The roll of honour included even Wellington's chief engineer, Sir Richard Fletcher, who was killed at San Sebastian in 1813.

A view of the ditch at Ciudad Rodrigo, with the fausse braie on the left and the walls on the right. The Great Breach was located at the end of the walls on the right, where the ditch turns to the right. The fausse braie was also severely damaged and the repair work can clearly be seen close-up. Both the 5th and 94th advanced along this ditch, to attack the breach that lay at the end. The wall on the left is about 15 feet high and perhaps conveys something of the task facing the storming columns, who would have had to jump into the ditch before attacking the breach. The confusion in such places must have been great. Fortunately Ciudad Rodrigo fell relatively quickly, but it is easy to see how much carnage and chaos there must have been at Badajoz, in ditches such as these, with the defenders pouring down a rain of missiles and musketry into them.

The forward angle of the fausse braie in front of the Great Breach at Ciudad Rodrigo. This section of the fausse braie was badly damaged by Allied artillery in January 1812. The cathedral can be seen behind it.

The conduct of the siege operations in the Peninsula was probably the most unsatisfactory aspect of what was otherwise a very successful campaign, one of the most successful the British army has ever fought. Much of this has to do with poor preparations, poor equipment, a lack of heavy siege guns, no corps of trained sappers and miners and, more importantly, a woeful shortage of proper entrenching tools. Indeed, this latter shortfall was known to the French and at Badajoz, Governor Phillipon offered bounties for tools captured during the sorties made from the town. Wellington's army was also a very inexperienced one when it came to the business of sieges. In fact, commenting on the fall of Ciudad Rodrigo in January 1812 the great historian of the British army, Sir John Fortescue, said that, setting aside the wars in India it was the first time since Drogheda and Wexford had fallen in 1649 that a British army had successfully stormed a town of any importance. Monte Video, stormed in February 1807, hardly ranks as a town of great importance and boasted relatively weak fortifications whilst Buenos Aires, taken the previous year and attacked again in 1807, was an open town. Therefore, much of what Wellington's army did as regards siege operations was a combination of what might be termed a 'hands-on' approach and a result of observations made during the French sieges of the same fortresses.

There were two main requirements necessary for a satisfactory siege. The first was a force strong enough to be able to besiege the town from all sides, and strong enough to be able to prevent the garrison from being able to leave the town in order to get messages through to any friendly force. Second, a force was needed of sufficient strength to prevent any interference from any relieving force. A perfect example of the need for the latter arose at Badajoz in May 1811 when Beresford, engaged in the first siege of the town, had to break off the siege in order to meet Soult in the field at Albuera. Had he been at Badajoz in sufficient strength he would have been able to meet Soult without having to raise the siege. Fortunately, Wellington was able to meet both these requirements at Ciudad Rodrigo and Badajoz.

Once an army appeared before a town the engineers would set about determining the point or points of attack. The various weaknesses and strengths of a fortress would usually be apparent to both attacker and defender and any diligent garrison commander would almost certainly have constructed small forts upon those points that posed the greatest threat. At Ciudad Rodrigo, for example, a long, round hill called the Greater Teson overlooked the town, which is why the French built a small redoubt upon it. This would have to be taken before any parallels could be begun and breaching batteries sited. Part of the problem of defending the fortresses lay in their location. Most of the great fortresses in the Peninsula had been built long ago, some dating back to the days

**Robert Craufurd (1764-1812).
Controversial but brilliant,
Craufurd commanded first the
Light Brigade then the Light
Division in the Peninsula
between 1809 and 1812. His
'career of earthly glory' in the
Peninsula was dogged by a
series of unfortunate scrapes
although he remained one of the
finest commanders Wellington
possessed. Indeed, after
Craufurd's death at Ciudad
Rodrigo, Wellington was moved
to call it 'a great blow'.**

of the wars between the Moors and Christians. Without the threat of artillery, hills such as the Greater Teson at Ciudad Rodrigo were never considered to be of any threat. However, with the introduction of gunpowder and heavy artillery these geographic features suddenly became the potential source of much danger, hence the small forts. There was also a widespread modernisation of many fortresses, both in the Peninsula and throughout Europe, largely as a result of principles of defence and siegecraft laid down in the 17th and 18th centuries by the great French engineer Vauban. It is interesting to note that the majority of walled towns in Spain that were never modernised, Avila for example, were never besieged in the way that either Ciudad Rodrigo or Badajoz were, because they were so weak in terms of fortifications that they would have been virtually indefensible. Then there were works called outworks. These were small forts of varying strength and design which were again constructed on weak points, although they differed from the usual forts inasmuch as they were much closer to the fortresses' walls and were often connected to them. At Badajoz there were three outworks, the forts Pardaleras, Picurina and San Roque. We will come on to the detail of Badajoz's fortifications and defences in due course.

Once a town had been encircled and the point of attack established, the besiegers would break ground, that is to say they would begin construction of the first parallel. This was usually sited out of range of the garrison's artillery as the working parties would be working in the open without any real means of protection. The idea was to dig a parallel and pile up the spoil as a sort of rampart, of sufficient thickness to be able to withstand enemy artillery. Thick ramparts were often enough to sustain the power of round shot although common shell and other explosive shells continued to cause casualties. Once the first parallel had been completed a sap or zig-zag would be dug forward and a second parallel dug. It was often in the second parallel that the breaching batteries were constructed. These batteries would often come under the most intense fire from the defenders as it would be from here that the real damage to the walls would be done. Also, it was the batteries that provided the only real covering fire for the working parties, although riflemen in Wellington's army were employed against the gunners on the walls of the town.

With the parallels dug, the breaching batteries constructed and the points of attack selected it was down to the skill of the artillery to blast away at the walls to effect a breach. And a skilful business it was. Anybody who has stood where Wellington's breaching batteries were sited at Ciudad Rodrigo, Badajoz and San Sebastian, for example, will have appreciated just how small a target the gunners would have had from their often distant positions. And it was not simply a case of blasting away in a haphazard manner against the walls. No, the guns were trained to fire at the base of the walls. In theory, this would eventually bring the wall crashing down into the ditch and by so doing would, hopefully, create a sort of ramp up which the stormers would be able to attack. Naturally, the defenders would do their best to clear away the rubbish and prevent this. They would also make sure that the breach, when practicable (i.e. passable), was blocked by as many deadly devices as their imagination, ingenuity and resources would allow. The favourite device was the chevaux-de-frise, a long piece of timber with sharp sword blades, spikes and other sharp objects protruding from it. This would be chained to the ground and, as would be the case at Badajoz, would prove impassable to the attacking troops.

As well as trying to preserve the defences and clear away the debris, a good governor of a fortress would ensure that he carried out a vigorous defence and not simply sit and wait for the assault to begin. A good commander would carry out sorties to damage the besieger's works, carry off their tools and do as much material damage as was possible. Trenches would be filled in and prisoners carried off; anything, in fact, to retard the siege operation. As well as having a practical side it had two other purposes. First, it maintained morale amongst the garrison who, from being on the defensive, could actually take the offensive from time to time. Second, these sorties and raids bought valuable time for the garrison. After all, it was unlikely that a garrison would be simply abandoned to its fate. Therefore, the longer the siege wore on the more likelihood there was of relief. As we shall see, Badajoz provides us with a perfect example of a garrison turning an apparently hopeless position into a race against time for the besiegers.

A breach was deemed 'practicable' by the engineers once they had decided that it was possible for attacking troops to pass through it, whereupon the besieging commander would summon the garrison to surrender. If it did, the garrison would march out with the honours of war, albeit into captivity. If, however, it chose to fight on, it ran the risk of being put to the sword. This was in keeping with the convention of the day, but Napoleon had nevertheless decreed that his garrison commanders should never surrender a fortress without first having sustained at least one assault. The ethics of a storm is a very complex subject and is a point which we shall deal with later in this book. The actual assault would be preceded by a 'Forlorn Hope', a small group of volunteers who knew they risked almost certain death. It was, nevertheless, a task which never lacked volunteers, mainly due to the fact that it could provide promotion for any fortunate survivors. The main storming columns would be guided by engineers while men carrying grassbags led the way, the bags to be thrown into the ditches in order to facilitate the stormers' descent. The rest was in the lap of the gods. With good planning and execution, and plenty of good fortune, a successful storming was possible. If not, heavy casualties and potentially catastrophic defeat were certain. As we shall see, at Badajoz it was a very fine line between victory and defeat. Wellington may have considered Waterloo a close run thing, but the storming of Badajoz was equally close.

CIUDAD RODRIGO

Having gathered together the necessary tools, equipment and siege impedimenta, Wellington's army marched east from its camps on the western bank of the river Agueda and appeared before Ciudad Rodrigo on 8 January 1812. The town itself stands on a low hill situated on the right or northern bank of the river Agueda. In fact, the river runs north-west to south-east and is spanned by an old Roman bridge close to the south-western angle of the town. Overlooking the bridge is a Moorish castle, giving the defenders complete control of it. Therefore, Wellington's men had constructed a trestle bridge which was laid across the Agueda at Marialva, a couple of miles to the north-west. The walls, just over thirty feet high, were a mixture of medieval and moorish origin but they had been modernised in accordance with Vauban's principles. There are no bastions at Ciudad Rodrigo but the walls were encircled by a strong ditch divided along its entire length by a fausse braie, that is to

'A View of the Storming and Taking of Ciudad Rodrigo in Spain'. A contemporary print depicting the events of 19 January 1812 when the town was stormed. The principal features of the assault are shown, but in a haphazard way. For example, the Light Division are attacking the breach on the left, with the 94th shown coming on behind them. Also, Mackinnon is blown up in the centre, while behind him is the suburb of San Francisco, which is in the wrong place.

CIUDAD RODRIGO, 8 – 19 JANUARY, 1812

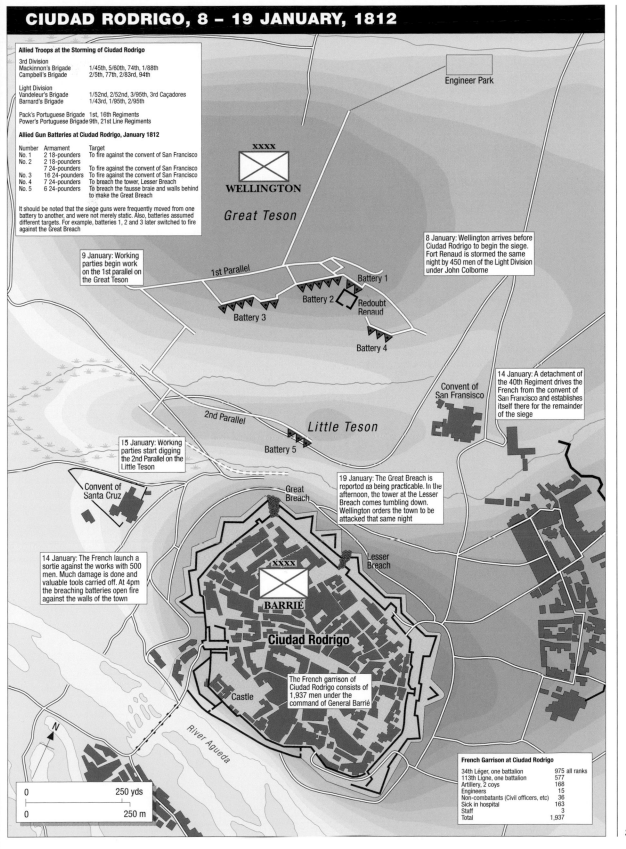

Allied Troops at the Storming of Ciudad Rodrigo

3rd Division
Mackinnon's Brigade   1/45th, 5/60th, 74th, 1/88th
Campbell's Brigade   2/5th, 77th, 2/83rd, 94th

Light Division
Vandeleur's Brigade   1/52nd, 2/52nd, 3/95th, 3rd Caçadores
Barnard's Brigade   1/43rd, 1/95th, 2/95th

Pack's Portuguese Brigade   1st, 16th Regiments
Power's Portuguese Brigade 9th, 21st Line Regiments

Allied Gun Batteries at Ciudad Rodrigo, January 1812

Number	Armament	Target
No. 1	2 18-pounders	To fire against the convent of San Francisco
No. 2	2 18-pounders	
	7 24-pounders	To fire against the convent of San Francisco
No. 3	16 24-pounders	To fire against the convent of San Francisco
No. 4	7 24-pounders	To breach the tower, Lesser Breach
No. 5	6 24-pounders	To breach the fausse braie and walls behind to make the Great Breach

It should be noted that the siege guns were frequently moved from one battery to another, and were not merely static. Also, batteries assumed different targets. For example, batteries 1, 2 and 3 later switched to fire against the Great Breach

XXXX
WELLINGTON

Great Teson

Engineer Park

8 January: Wellington arrives before Ciudad Rodrigo to begin the siege. Fort Renaud is stormed the same night by 450 men of the Light Division under John Colborne

9 January: Working parties begin work on the 1st parallel on the Great Teson

1st Parallel

Battery 1
Battery 2
Redoubt Renaud
Battery 3
Battery 4

Convent of San Fransisco

14 January: A detachment of the 40th Regiment drives the French from the convent of San Francisco and establishes itself there for the remainder of the siege

2nd Parallel

Little Teson

15 January: Working parties start digging the 2nd Parallel on the Little Teson

Battery 5

19 January: The Great Breach is reported as being practicable. In the afternoon, the tower at the Lesser Breach comes tumbling down. Wellington orders the town to be attacked that same night

Convent of Santa Cruz

Great Breach

Lesser Breach

14 January: The French launch a sortie against the works with 500 men. Much damage is done and valuable tools carried off. At 4pm the breaching batteries open fire against the walls of the town

XXXX
BARRIÉ

Ciudad Rodrigo

Castle

The French garrison of Ciudad Rodrigo consists of 1,937 men under the command of General Barrié

River Agueda

N

0   250 yds
0   250 m

French Garrison at Ciudad Rodrigo

34th Léger, one battalion	975 all ranks
113th Ligne, one battalion	577
Artillery, 2 coys	168
Engineers	15
Non-combatants (Civil officers, etc)	36
Sick in hospital	163
Staff	3
Total	1,937

31

Another contemporary print, again showing the main features but in the wrong order. In this print, Craufurd is mortally wounded (right), with Mackinnon being blown up away to the left; it should be round the other way.

say, a strong earth bank. This meant, of course, that Wellington's artillery would have to breach the fausse braie as well as the walls themselves. Owing to the river to the south-west of the town and the high hill upon which it stood, the place could only really be attacked from the north. Therefore, the ditches and fausse braie only covered about three-quarters of the town's walls.

The town's vulnerable spot was obvious to all. It was a length of wall about two hundred yards in length situated along the northern sector of the town. Here, the walls are overlooked by a long, oval-shaped hill called the Greater Teson, which lies about six hundred yards further north and which, more significantly, is thirteen feet higher than the walls. Anybody in possession of the Greater Teson would have a clear view of the walls. Even today, it is possible to look straight out across to the walls in spite of the blocks of flats that have been built on the Lesser Teson, a smaller hill situated about halfway between the Greater Teson and the walls of the town. The glacis, which would normally afford the walls a certain amount of protection, was rendered almost useless by the occupation of the Greater Teson as any guns situated upon it would have an easy task of firing over it against the walls. The French knew perfectly well that Wellington would break ground on the Greater Teson and had constructed a small redoubt mounting two cannons and a howitzer, called Fort Renaud after the town's former governor, who had been captured by the Spanish guerrilla Julian Sanchez. There were also two fortified convents, Santa Cruz and San Francisco, which would have to be taken before the main assault.

The capture of Ciudad Rodrigo would, of course, give Wellington command of the northern corridor between Spain and Portugal, but there was another prize that lurked within the town's walls, for Marmont had thrown into the place the siege train of the Army of Portugal complete with artillery and ammunition. The garrison itself numbered around 1,800 men, the bulk of which were from the 34th Light and 133rd Line Regiments. There was also a number of Italians in the garrison who would suffer severely when the town was stormed. Governor of the town was General Barrié, of whom Fortescue quotes Marmont as considering him, 'a detestable officer, endowed neither with vigilance nor with resolution'.

Wellington's engineers were quick to spot the point of attack and the direction from where it should come. It was the same place from where Ney had besieged the town in 1810 and was, of course, the Greater Teson. The location selected for the breach was at the north-western angle of the walls, the point nearest to the Allied trenches. But before the first parallel could be opened Wellington had to capture the redoubt on the Greater Teson, Fort Renaud. With this in his hands Wellington would have a commanding view of the whole of the northern face of Ciudad Rodrigo.

Wellington was determined to have Ciudad Rodrigo as quickly as possible and decided to take Fort Renaud on the very first night, 8 January. The task was given to ten companies of the Light Division under Colonel John Colborne, later to become Lord Seaton, whose exploits with the 52nd at Waterloo had a great bearing on that battle. Having formed his men on the northern side of the Greater Teson, Colborne's men made their way forward in the dark, crossing the wide, open top of the hill before arriving on the glacis of the fort itself. Scaling ladders were quickly thrown into the ditch, whilst four companies threw themselves down upon the glacis and opened fire on the defenders, who managed to get off just one round from a gun before Colborne's men were in the ditch. The defenders threw grenades into the ditch, causing some loss amongst the attackers, but the men of the Light Division were not to be denied. The fort was quickly surrounded and it did not take long for Colborne's men to break into it, the defenders being overwhelmed, only four managing to escape out of a garrison of about 50. Three French soldiers were killed whilst the remainder were taken prisoner. Therefore, at a cost of just 6 dead and 20 wounded Wellington had cleared the top of the Greater Teson and he could now concentrate on opening up the first parallel, although he would have to wait until

The Roman bridge over the Agueda at Ciudad Rodrigo. It was across this bridge that O'Toole made his attack with the Portuguese 2nd Caçadores and the light company of the 2/83rd to silence the two guns placed beneath the castle. The modern bridge can be seen to the right.

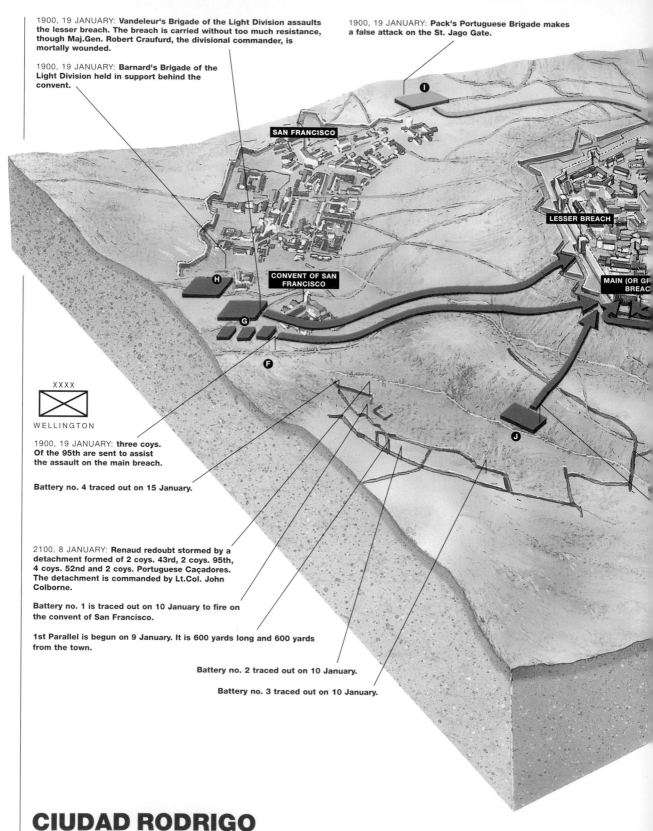

1900, 19 JANUARY: **Vandeleur's Brigade of the Light Division assaults the lesser breach. The breach is carried without too much resistance, though Maj.Gen. Robert Craufurd, the divisional commander, is mortally wounded.**

1900, 19 JANUARY: **Pack's Portuguese Brigade makes a false attack on the St. Jago Gate.**

1900, 19 JANUARY: **Barnard's Brigade of the Light Division held in support behind the convent.**

SAN FRANCISCO

LESSER BREACH

CONVENT OF SAN FRANCISCO

MAIN (OR GR BREACH

XXXX

WELLINGTON

1900, 19 JANUARY: **three coys. Of the 95th are sent to assist the assault on the main breach.**

Battery no. 4 traced out on 15 January.

2100, 8 JANUARY: **Renaud redoubt stormed by a detachment formed of 2 coys. 43rd, 2 coys. 95th, 4 coys. 52nd and 2 coys. Portuguese Caçadores. The detachment is commanded by Lt.Col. John Colborne.**

Battery no. 1 is traced out on 10 January to fire on the convent of San Francisco.

1st Parallel is begun on 9 January. It is 600 yards long and 600 yards from the town.

Battery no. 2 traced out on 10 January.

Battery no. 3 traced out on 10 January.

CIUDAD RODRIGO
The Siege and Storming, 8-19 January 1812

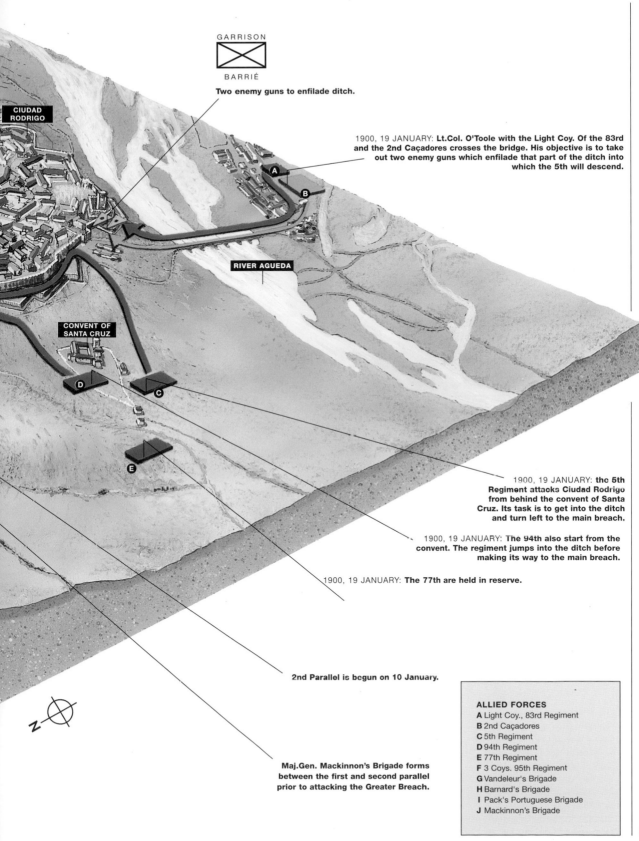

GARRISON

BARRIÉ

Two enemy guns to enfilade ditch.

CIUDAD RODRIGO

1900, 19 JANUARY: **Lt.Col. O'Toole with the Light Coy. Of the 83rd and the 2nd Caçadores crosses the bridge. His objective is to take out two enemy guns which enfilade that part of the ditch into which the 5th will descend.**

A

B

RIVER AGUEDA

CONVENT OF SANTA CRUZ

D

C

E

1900, 19 JANUARY: **the 5th Regiment attacks Ciudad Rodrigo from behind the convent of Santa Cruz. Its task is to get into the ditch and turn left to the main breach.**

1900, 19 JANUARY: **The 94th also start from the convent. The regiment jumps into the ditch before making its way to the main breach.**

1900, 19 JANUARY: **The 77th are held in reserve.**

2nd Parallel is begun on 10 January.

N

Maj.Gen. Mackinnon's Brigade forms between the first and second parallel prior to attacking the Greater Breach.

ALLIED FORCES
A Light Coy., 83rd Regiment
B 2nd Caçadores
C 5th Regiment
D 94th Regiment
E 77th Regiment
F 3 Coys. 95th Regiment
G Vandeleur's Brigade
H Barnard's Brigade
I Pack's Portuguese Brigade
J Mackinnon's Brigade

Major-General Henry Mackinnon, killed while leading the attack on the Great Breach at Ciudad Rodrigo. Mackinnon's badly charred body was found on the ramparts the morning after the storm and was taken to Espeja for burial by his regiment, the Coldstream Guards. Mackinnon's memoirs, *A Journal of the Campaign in Portugal and Spain*, were published posthumously in 1812, for the benefit of his young sons. He was the uncle of Dan Mackinnon, later to be one of the defenders of Hougoumont, who was famous throughout Wellington's army for his practical jokes, which included his impersonating the Duke of York, a joke which earned him a censure from Wellington.

The Moorish castle at Ciudad Rodrigo. Now a luxury hotel, the castle witnessed the surrender of General Barrié after the storming on 19 January 1812. The two guns, which were silenced by O'Toole, were situated in what is now the garden, on the bottom right of this photo.

daylight as the French, once they saw the fort had fallen, opened up a concentrated fire upon it.

9 January passed with little activity, other than at the fort, which was strengthened. A communication trench was also started across the Teson down the rear or northern slope of the hill to the open ground beyond where the engineers established their park. The first parallel was finally opened during the night of 9 January , it being the same one the French had used when they had besieged Ciudad Rodrigo in 1810. This made the task appreciably easier but it was still an unpleasant business as the weather was bitterly cold and each of the four divisions that took turns digging – the 1st, 3rd, 4th and Light – spent twenty-fours hours in the trenches, exposed to both the elements and enemy fire.

The digging progressed slowly owing to the dreadful freezing conditions in the trenches. French gunners situated along the northern walls of the town found the exact range of the parallels and kept up a destructive and annoying fire on the working parties, consisting of around 1,000 men per shift. Even the 'Gentlemen's Sons' – the two regiments of Foot Guards – were not spared the rigours of siege warfare.

The site of the Lesser Breach at Ciudad Rodrigo. This picture was taken in 1994, before restoration work took place, and clearly shows how poor a state the wall was in. In 1812, a tower stood here before it collapsed after being shelled by British artillery. Robert Craufurd lies buried beneath this wall.

Indeed, John Mills, of the Coldstream Guards, made some acute observations of the conditions and left a vivid account of his own experiences. 'We stole along the open ground till we came within three hundred yards of the town, when the ground was measured out and we set to work. The fire from the batteries had slackened as the night approached, but no sooner did they hear our pick-axes at work than they threw a fire ball which fell about 20 yards in our front and threw out such a light that they could see every button on our coats. The ball burnt for twenty minutes during which time we lay on our faces to hide ourselves, and they fired most gloriously. When the light was burnt out we set to work, and before daylight completed our battery, as did the others. Before the sun rose we skulked out and remained out of shot till we were relieved by the 4th Division. We then marched here [the Guards' camp at Espeja] and got in at four o'clock, having been thirty-four hours in the open air, with no shelter, in the most biting frost, so hard that the water froze in the men's canteens'. It was, therefore, a bad and unpleasant business, but with no sappers and miners at his disposal Wellington had to rely on the brawn of the infantry.

We may well wonder what Marmont was doing whilst the early stages of the siege wore on. Well, he was doing very little. In fact, he had no knowledge whatsoever of the siege having begun until 15 January. This is not as remarkable as it seems as Barrié's messages, sent to Governor Thiébault at Salamanca, were intercepted by the marauding bands of guerrillas. Therefore, amazing as it seems given the relatively short distance between Ciudad Rodrigo and Salamanca, Marmont, who was marching north to Valladolid, was in complete ignorance of the perilous situation in which Barrié found himself.

The siege wore on and by the evening of 13 January the batteries were ready to accommodate the siege guns. These heavy guns, 18- and 24-pounders, were huge beasts, capable of firing about twenty times an hour and after each firing the guns had to be dragged back eight feet to their positions after recoiling. Firing at night time was considered a waste of ammunition and so the artillery worked during daylight only, although even then it was not always easy to see the target. At Ciudad Rodrigo, for example, heavy fog and morning mists meant that the guns could not be fired at all on some days.

On 13 January 300 men of the 5/60th and the King's German Legion stormed the convent of Santa Cruz which allowed Wellington to sap forward and begin another parallel along the Lesser Teson. Also, 27 guns were placed in their batteries in preparation for the barrage which would, hopefully, bring down the walls at the selected places. At around 10am on 14 January, however, the operation suffered a setback when about 500 French troops issued from the town and made a sortie into the besiegers' trenches, filling in large sections and carrying off valuable tools. The sortie was well planned and executed, although the French were assisted by a flaw in the besiegers' arrangements. What happened when each shift finished its spell of duty int the trenches was that the shift and its guards would file out and march away, leaving the trenches unmanned until the incoming shift entered to begin its spell. The French had an observation post in the tower of the cathedral and this procedure was clearly visible to them. It took no military genius, therefore, to see that the changing of shifts was the time to make a sortie. Although the works were damaged no guns were spiked, owing to the vigilance of some of the workmen who manned the batteries and when General Graham advanced with the relieving division the French took off, satisfied with their morning's work.

Towards the late afternoon on 14 January the breaching batteries finally opened up with a tremendous roar as the 24-pound shots were hurled through the air at the walls. Unfortunately, it was quickly discovered that the batteries had been sited too far forward and that it was not possible to see the bottom of the walls, which was the actual target. Instead, the balls smashed into the walls too high up. Much time was lost in re-siting the guns, although while this went on two guns were trained on the convent of San Francisco and succeeded in

Major-General Robert Craufurd leads his Light Division against the lesser Breach at Ciudad Rodrigo on the night of 19 January 1812. The men entered the town without too much difficulty but Craufurd himself, standing in full view of the defenders, was mortally wounded by a musket shot. He died on 23 January and was buried beneath the breach that was stormed by his men.

driving out the garrison there. At length, the breaching batteries resumed their fire, causing severe damage to the walls and the fausse braie. On the 15th it was decided to make a second breach, the target being a small tower which protruded from the walls just in front of the cathedral. By dawn on the 16th, all was ready to begin firing at the new target but a dense fog came down and brought a halt to all firing. Instead, Wellington made use of the time by sending forward parties of riflemen, who dug themselves into rifle pits before the walls. From here, they would be able to direct a well-aimed fire at the defenders visible in the embrasures. For a trained marksmen of the 95th, armed with the Baker rifle, this presented no real challenge.

The firing resumed at midday on 17 January, the defenders replying with everything they had. However, despite their efforts, they could do nothing to prevent the main breach being made in the walls at the north-

Ciudad Rodrigo the day after the storming. This contemporary print shows a couple of British officers viewing the scene after the storming. Note the damage done to the fausse braie at the main breach on the right. Note also that no damage has been done to the fausse braie at the Great Breach, away to the left. This very accurate picture also gives a good impression of the damage done to the buildings immediately behind the breaches.

west angle of the town. This was judged by the engineers to be 'practicable', that is to say open, by the evening of the 18th. And even as his engineers reported upon the state of the main breach, the tower that had been selected as the location for the second breach came crashing down into the ditch in front of it, and by daybreak on the 19th the gap had been much enlarged. Thus, by the evening of 18 January, Wellington was presented with two breaches, one much larger than the other, in the walls of Ciudad Rodrigo. His summons for the town to surrender having been rejected by Barrié, Wellington took himself off to one of the forward saps and sat down to write his orders for the coming assault.

Wellington's arrangements for the assault ran to sixteen detailed paragraphs. The attack was to begin at 7pm that same evening, the 19th, and involved two main attacks. Major-General Henry Mackinnon's brigade of the 3rd Division, supported by the Portuguese brigade of the same division, would assault the Great Breach directly from the Lesser Teson. Another column, consisting of the 5th Regiment, with the 77th Regiment in reserve, would form behind the convent of Santa Cruz and advance, entering the ditch beneath the castle before turning to their left, clearing away any enemy posts between them and the main breach. The 94th Regiment was also to advance from the Santa Cruz, entering the ditch just to the right of the main breach before turning to the left, which would bring the regiment to the main breach. Major-General Vandeleur's brigade of the Light Division would tackle the Lesser Breach, supported by Barnard's brigade of the same division. Meanwhile, on the opposite side of the river Agueda, the 2nd Caçadores and the Light Company of the 83rd, under Colonel O'Toole, were to cross the Roman bridge and make an attack on the small outwork in front of the castle, the object being the destruction of two guns placed so as to cover the entrance of the ditch just below the castle. A false attack by Denis Pack's brigade would take place on the St Jago Gate, situated on the south-east side of the town. All of the attacking columns would be guided to their respective points of attack by Royal Engineers.

In June 1811, Wellington's men had assaulted Fort San Christobal at Badajoz but without success. This, however, was the first time in the Peninsula that Wellington himself had presided over a large-scale attack on a major town. It was to be both a momentous and memorable night but, in comparison with the attack on Badajoz twelve weeks later, it was to prove a relatively small and straightforward affair. As already stated in an earlier chapter, this was to be the first time a major fortified town had been stormed by a British army since 1649 and as such nobody quite knew what to expect. Of course, each man knew he stood a good chance of being struck down, particularly if he was one of the Forlorn Hope, the almost suicidal squad of volunteers who preceded the main storming columns. No man shrank from the task, however, and when Picton and Craufurd assembled their respective divisions – the 3rd and Light – they did so amidst an air of great expectancy.

As darkness fell on the bitterly cold night of 19 January, Craufurd's Light Division assembled behind the convent of San Francisco. Here, the brilliant but controversial Craufurd turned to his beloved division and addressed them for what was to prove the last time. 'Soldiers,' he shouted, 'the eyes of your country are upon you. Be steady, be cool, be firm in the assault. The town must be yours this night. Once masters of the wall, let your first duty be to clear the ramparts, and in doing this keep together. Now lads, for the breach!' With this short but stirring address, Craufurd, known as 'Black Bob' for his fiery temper, led his men into action for the last time. The Light Division had to cross about 500 yards of open, moonlit ground before it approached the fausse braie, behind which was the Lesser Breach.

As soon as the men carrying the grassbags reached the ditch they threw the bags into it, which made it easier for the stormers to jump down without injury. Ladders were placed in the ditch also, down which the men quickly scrambled. However, as soon as they began to fill the ditch

A view from the top of the Moorish castle, looking towards the cathedral. The Greater Teson is the open space on the left centre, just visible above the houses.

the French, who were waiting patiently for the right moment, opened fire. The ditch was very quickly a seething mass of British troops, struggling in the darkness to find their way to the breach. Grenades were tossed into the ditch by the French and the whole scene was illuminated by the flash and glare of musketry and explosions. In the confusion, some of the Light Division made for a damaged ravelin and suffered heavily before the mistake was realised. George Napier, one of the three famous Napier brothers, was shot down as were a good many others. But up on the glacis, across the ditch from the Lesser Breach, the greatest casualty was to occur. There, standing in full view to the French, was Robert Craufurd, urging his men forward, 'at the highest pitch of his voice'. The orange light of the explosions around him almost certainly revealed him to the French and, while his men began to climb the breach, he was struck down by a musket ball which passed through his arm, broke his ribs, passed through his lungs and lodged in or close to his spine. The force of the blow sent him spinning backwards down the glacis and for a short time he lay alone, exposed to the fire of the defenders, until his ADC, James Kennedy, dragged him away to a safer spot. Vandeleur had also been struck down and command of the Light Division fell upon Andrew Barnard. His men soon gained the breach and, turning to their right, began to clear the ramparts as far as the Greater Breach.

The other attacks met with similar success. O'Toole's Portuguese and the 83rd crossed the bridge over the Agueda and did a fine job in silencing the two guns beneath the castle, thus saving the 5th and 77th from any embarassment. These latter two regiments, meanwhile, sallied out from the Santa Cruz and forced their way into the ditch, hacking down the gate and the palisades which barred their way, under heavy fire before making their way to the Greater Breach. Campbell and the 94th had likewise left their jumping-off point at the Santa Cruz and had entered the ditch to the left of the 5th and 77th. Campbell, in fact, has good claim to be the first to reach the top of the breach, for having clawed his way over the debris which marked the fausse braie, he found the 5th and 77th in a similar situation, gazing up in the dark at the main breach which yawned above them. Campbell struggled to the top of the

One of the forts thrown up by Wellington on the Greater Teson after the storming of Ciudad Rodrigo. This is the smaller of the two forts.

RIGHT The view from the larger of the two forts on the Greater Teson thrown up by Wellington after the capture of Ciudad Rodrigo. In the middle distance can be seen the smaller fort, while the town itself can be seen further on. John Mills, of the Coldstream Guards, records that there were four such forts, named Wellington, Mackinnon, Craufurd and Castaños, although traces of only two can be found today.

The ditch in front of the larger fort upon the Greater Teson at Ciudad Rodrigo. The height from the ditch to the top of the rampart on the right is about 30 feet and in wet weather fills with water, thus creating a substantial defence. The fort lies about 200 yards to the north of the smaller fort.

breach only to find his way barred by a drop of around sixteen feet into the town, whilst the breach itself had been retrenched by two ditches, ten feet deep and as many wide. Fortunately, the French had left some planks of wood across their retrenchments, over which Campbell's men very obligingly dashed.

Even as Campbell's men began crossing the planks, Henry Mackinnon came up, leading his brigade of the 3rd Division into the Greater Breach. No sooner had the men torn their way to the top than the French exploded a huge mine, which cast both friend and foe alike hundreds of feet into the air. Sadly, Mackinnon was one of them and his blackened body was found on the ramparts the following morning. His men continued pouring up into the breach, however, but received heavy casualties from two guns mounted in the left rear of the breach which swept it with a vicious crossfire. It was at this point that a group of men from the 74th and 88th Regiments put down their muskets and, armed with just their bayonets, climbed up across the breach and made for the two guns. The gunners stood by their guns but were put to death by the enraged Rangers and soon afterwards the 3rd Division was pouring into the town, the defenders giving way before it.

With the silencing of the two guns at the top of the breach, all serious resistance ended and the 3rd Division, with the 94th, 5th and 77th, passed down into the streets of the town. The Light Division had already entered, whilst on the other side of town Pack's Portuguese had broken in also. Ciudad Rodrigo was finally in Allied hands and Governor Barrié made his way to the castle, where he surrendered soon afterwards to Lieutenant John Gurwood of the 52nd, although Lieutenant Mackie, of the 88th, was later championed by the 3rd Division as being the first to take the governor.

The capture of Ciudad Rodrigo by Wellington's men was a great achievement, but this was somewhat tarnished by their behaviour afterwards. Nobody had issued clear instructions as to the procedure in the event of a successful storming and Wellington's officers were left to grope around in the darkness to try to maintain or restore order in the narrow streets of the town. Some units did stay together but others, free from the shackles of army discipline, embarked on an orgy of plundering, breaking into successive houses in search of food and drink. A few buildings were set on fire and many civilians abused. Some officers were likewise assaulted as they tried to restore order and for a few hours Ciudad Rodrigo was a very dangerous place. Moreover, there was still a sizeable French garrison to be dealt with, although it appears never to have occurred to them to attempt a counter attack during the disorder following the fall of the town. Gradually, the tumult died down, the men began to return to their camps and at daylight order was finally restored. However, the experience was not lost on Wellington's men and as we shall see it was a major factor in the massive outbreak of disorder following the storming of Badajoz.

The capture of Ciudad Rodrigo after just eleven days of open trenches was a great achievement for Wellington's army, coming as it did in the middle of winter, with an army inexperienced and ill-equipped for siege warfare, and with large French forces not a million miles away, although the Emperor himself had not helped their situation with a series of ill-advised and meddlesome orders. In fact, Napoleon's hand in affairs in Spain was often to the detriment of the French as he appears never to have had a grip on the reality of the situation there. Those reports that were fortunate enough to elude the marauding bands of Spaniards and reach Paris were often outdated by the time they arrived and when Napoleon's own orders in turn reached his marshals in Spain the situation had often changed drastically. The constant bickering and petty jealousies of the various marshals did the French no favours either. All this conspired to give Wellington the opportunity to sieze Ciudad Rodrigo, an achievement which moved even Marmont to write, 'Never was such an operation pushed forward with the like activity'.

The siege and storming of Ciudad Rodrigo cost Wellington 9 officers killed and 70 wounded, whilst 186 men were killed and 846 wounded. Of these, 59 officers and 503 men became casualties during the actual storming. The French lost 8 officers killed and 21 wounded, with about 500 men killed and wounded. A further 60 officers and 1,300 men taken prisoner. Amongst the Allied casualties was Robert Craufurd, who had been mortally wounded whilst urging his men into the Lesser Breach. Craufurd's story can be found elsewhere in the histories of the Peninsular War and space precludes any deep discussion of either his life or his methods. Suffice to say that when he died on 23 January, after lingering in great pain for four days, Wellington was moved to call it 'the bitterest blow of the war', a fact borne out by the imposing funeral afforded to the finest commander of light troops the Allied army possessed. Another notable casualty was Henry Mackinnon, uncle of Dan Mackinnon, the great joker of the British army. Mackinnon was found dead on the ramparts of Ciudad Rodrigo on the morning of 20 January and was taken by his regiment, the Coldstream Guards, to Espeja for burial.

THE MARCH SOUTH

With both Almeida and Ciudad Rodrigo in his hands, Wellington had a firm grip on the northern route between Spain and Portugal and he could begin to make plans to move south and lay siege to Badajoz. He issued orders for the movement of stores from Setubal to Elvas, where the siege train would assemble. The heavy siege guns used at Ciudad Rodrigo were removed to Almeida and from there to Barca d'Alva. From here they would be taken by boat to Oporto, by sea to Setubal and finally by road to Elvas. Sixteen heavy howitzers were sent overland by way of Villa Velha whilst twenty 18-pounders would be lent by Admiral Berkeley at Lisbon for the purpose of assisting in the siege of Badajoz. Unfortunately, these naval guns turned out to be Russian guns which would not accommodate the normal British shot. Fortunately, Wellington was blessed with a fine chief artilleryman, Alexander Dickson, who managed to scour the Lisbon arsenals for a mixture of both Russian and Portuguese shot, both of which fitted the Russian guns rather well.

With arrangements for the transportation of stores, supplies, guns and ammunition having been satisfactorily issued and implemented, Wellington began to move his troops south. Wellington himself did nothing but remained at his headquarters at Freneida in order to mislead the French into believing there would be no further offensive operations until the spring at the earliest. Alten's 1st Hussars of the

A view of the ramparts and ditch of Fort San Christobal, which lies on the northern bank of the Guadiana. It was against this fort that Wellington directed his efforts in June 1811 in an attack that went disastrously wrong. The defenders simply rolled grenades and barrels of gunpowder into the ditch below, which, filled as it was with British troops, was a very simple but deadly effective mode of defence.

King's German Legion remained behind also with units of Portuguese and Spanish cavalry to help mislead the French. One by one, Wellington's divisions began to move south until by 26 February virtually all of his infantry was on the move south towards Badajoz, with only the 5th Division delaying its departure. The move did not go completely undetected, however, for Marmont received news of the southward movement on 22 February, not that there was anything he could do to threaten Ciudad Rodrigo after Wellington's departure, for his siege train had been captured intact inside the town and, even without British infantry, Castaños, who assumed command of Ciudad Rodrigo, was quite capable of holding the place against the French. Nevertheless, Wellington delayed his departure from Freneida until the last possible moment as he knew it be the cue for the French to advance from Salamanca. Finally, with his army having moved south and seeing little point in delaying any longer, Wellington and his headquarters staff left Freneida on the afternoon of 5 March and six days later established new headquarters at Elvas, where preparations for the siege of Badajoz were pressing ahead.

The arrival of Wellington at Elvas brought a greater sense of urgency to the siege preparations. Gabions and fascines, essential for the protection of troops working in the trenches, were made in abundance, ladders were fashioned either from timbers and trees or, as was the case at Ciudad Rodrigo, from old wagons and carriages. Stores were accumulated and a large consignment of cutting tools delivered from the arsenal at Lisbon. We are indebted to Jones, the historian of the sieges, for listing the tools and stores ordered up for the siege of Badajoz (See pages 24–25). Arrangements were made also for the transportation of two bridges, one a flying bridge to be fixed over the Guadiana about a mile and a half above Badajoz and the other a pontoon bridge, formed of 22 pontoons, which was thown over the river about ten miles below it.

On 15 March, with all arrangements having been completed, Wellington moved his army forward and the following day William Carr Beresford, at the head of some 12,000 men of the 3rd, 4th and Light Divisions, with one squadron of Portuguese cavalry, crossed the

A view of the ditch from the ramparts at fort San Christobal, Badajoz.

Guadiana before closing in on Badajoz. There was little to dispute their approach, Phillipon contenting himself with sending out a few patrols to keep a watchful eye over their guests. In fact, it is possible that Phillipon was not unduly worried by the prospect of the coming siege. After all, he had made a very brave and successful defence of Badajoz the previous year, since when the town had been strengthened considerably. He had a strong and experienced garrison and was well stock with supplies. Furthermore, he knew of the relatively close proximity of French forces under Soult and Marmont

The glacis of Fort San Christobal, Badajoz. From this photo it is possible to see just how effective the glacis was here and the way it protects the walls, which, from this angle, are not visible.

who would surely come to his aid before Wellington had time to prise the town from him. Hence, he could be forgiven for appearing optimistic at his prospects. He was, however, to be proved sadly wrong for what he did not know was that Napoleon's orders from Paris prevented Marmont's moving to assist him until 27 March, by which time it would be too late.

The nearest French troops to Badajoz were two divisions under D'Erlon, but these would take weeks to gather together in order to act. Soult was likewise in the south, but he was occupied watching Ballasteros around Cadiz and Gibraltar. In fact, Soult would have to relinquish his grip on Grenada and the lines before Cadiz if he were to muster his forces in sufficient strength to be able to interfere with Wellington's operations at Badajoz, and even if he did he would have to face Sir Thomas Graham, who had crossed the Guadiana on 16 March with the 1st, 6th and 7th Divisions. These were to act as the covering force to the south and would be more than a match for any French force marching to Phillipon's relief from that direction. Soult had tried such an operation less than a year before and had found himself face to face with Beresford at the bloodbath of Albuera. Dare he risk such another operation? No, the only real threat to Wellington lay with Marmont and the Army of Portugal, but, unknown to Wellington, Napoleon had ordered Marmont to concentrate around Salamanca in the misguided belief that a threat to Ciudad Rodrigo would force Wellington to raise the siege of Badajoz and return north. However, the Allied commander was not unduly worried by any threat to Ciudad Rodrigo as he knew that Marmont had neither siege train nor sufficient transport or supplies, having lost most of these when the town fell on 19 January. Phillipon's own fate rested squarely upon his own ability to be able to defend the town for as long as possible for even Wellington knew that he himself could not maintain the siege indefinitely, estimating that he had around three to four weeks before Marmont's crucial appearance.

THE SIEGE OF BADAJOZ

The crossing of the river Guadiana by Wellington's army signalled the beginning of the third siege of Badajoz and by the evening of 16 March all communication between the garrison and the rest of the French forces in Spain was cut. Graham's covering force moved into position to the south of Badajoz whilst the besieging force encircled the town in preparation for the siege proper.

The town of Badajoz lies on the south bank of the River Guadiana and is the capital of the province of Estremadura. At the outset of the Peninsular War it had a population of around 16,000 inhabitants but this had dwindled as the war had dragged on. Many of the richer families had left the town and with the re-appearance of Wellington's army those who had experienced the miseries of starvation and deprivation during the previous sieges, by both French and Allies, decided to pack up and leave also. As Phillipon's chief engineer, Colonel Lamare, later wrote, 'They quitted their homes in tears, and often looked back with regret on their

A view of Fort San Christobal, the scene of the failed attacks in June 1811. Wellington attacked the fort from the right, over hard and open ground. The walls are protected efficiently by the glacis at the bottom of the photo. The Roman bridge can be seen over the Guadiana with a modern bridge in the far distance.

'Badajos, on the Guadiana, as approached from Albuquerque and Elvas'. This very accurate print, executed in 1813, shows the town from the northern bank of the Guadiana. The Tête du Pont can be seen at the near end of the bridge with the gate of Las Palmas at the far end. Away to the right can be seen the walls of the San Vincente bastion. To the left, the castle enclosure, or alcazabar, can be seen. In the centre stands the cathedral.

unhappy city, which they saw was about to be exposed a third time to all the calamities inseperable from war.' In view of what happened after the storming, they were probably very wise to leave the place. It was a town that had gained an unfortunate reputation amongst Wellington's men, who viewed the inhabitants with suspicion. There were rumours that the inhabitants had assisted the garrison during the previous sieges, that they had been seen firing from the ramparts and that they were pro-French. Also, the bad treatment shown to the British wounded who had been left at Badajoz after the battle of Talavera in 1809 was well known amongst the men. The strong resistance shown during the siege in June 1811 and, as we shall see, the vigorous defence of the place during the coming siege only served to heighten the reputation of Badajoz as a place to be made example of. All in all, the British fighting man had developed a marked dislike of Badajoz and its people and the men who now began to besiege the place did so bearing a definite grudge and with the feeling that they had a score to settle. As we shall see, that score was settled in the most dramatic manner.

Wellington's men were under no illusions as to the extent of the task ahead of them and knew that Badajoz would be a much tougher nut to crack than Ciudad Rodrigo. The town's fortifications formed an enclosure of nine bastions, connected by huge walls. Bastion no. 1 was joined to the old Moorish alcazabar or castle enclosure, which itself acted as a sort of citadel at the north-east angle of the town. The northern face of the town faced out across the river Guadiana, which provided a natural obstacle on that side, rendering it virtually impossible to attack from that side. The walls on the northern side of the town were fairly low in comparison with the walls elsewhere. On the northern bank of the Guadiana stood three outworks; the Fort San Christobal, the Tête du Pont and the lunette Verlé, the latter being constructed only a short time previous to the siege. These works were linked to the town by way of an old Roman bridge and, in cases of emergency, by ferry between the town and the San Christobal. When the Allies laid siege to Badajoz in June 1811, their efforts were directed against Fort San Christobal and the castle. During the 1812 siege, however, the San Christobal was to play only a minor role in the story.

49

An aerial view of the northern bank of the Guadiana. This photo, taken in 1914, shows Fort San Christobal (1), which was the scene of the failed attacks by Wellington in June 1811. Further north stands the lunette Verlé (2), named after a French general killed at Albuera. The covered way (3) from the fort to the Roman bridge can also be seen, as can the two small fleches, built to prevent the enemy from firing along the length of the track. Today the area around the fort is covered with trees, while an extensive building programme occupies almost all of the left-hand third of this photo.

On the southern bank there were three more outworks: Fort Pardaleras, situated in front of bastions 4 and 5, Fort Picurina, situated in front of bastion no. 7, and the lunette San Roque which covered the communication to the gate of La Trinidad. Fort Pardaleras had been little more than a pile of rubbish when the French army took possession of the town in 1811, since when it had been vastly improved. The gorge was closed by a good loop-holed wall, the ditches deepened, and the curtain on the right had been raised in order to see in reverse the approaches against bastions numbers 1, 2 and 3 between the fort and the Guadiana. The powder magazine and a bomb-proof barrack for the commandant and his garrison were rebuilt on their former foundations. The covered way was repaired and newly palisaded and the fort generally given the strength and solidity to withstand assault, although it was never tested until the night of the main assault on 6 April. Fort Picurina, on the other hand, effectively barred Wellington's access to the point where he wished to establish his breaching batteries. Therefore it would need to be taken early on in the siege. It was a strong little fort, with a scarp which varied from 13 to 16 feet and was cut on very hard soil. The fort had a palisaded covered way and the gorge was closed with a single row of palisades also. The ditch had been deepened to increase the height of the walls at the same time. At the fort's salient angle the French had cut a counterscarp out of the rock and had established six small galleries, perpendicular to the faces of the fort, which were joined together to bring a reverse fire to flank the ditches and which could not be seen from any point. Small mines were placed beneath the glacis and the ramparts well stocked with a large number of shells and barrels of gunpowder, which would be rolled down amongst any attacking force.

When the French besieged Badajoz in 1811 they made a breach in the curtain wall between bastions 3 and 4. This had been repaired and the trenches used by them filled in. The ravelin between bastions 2 and

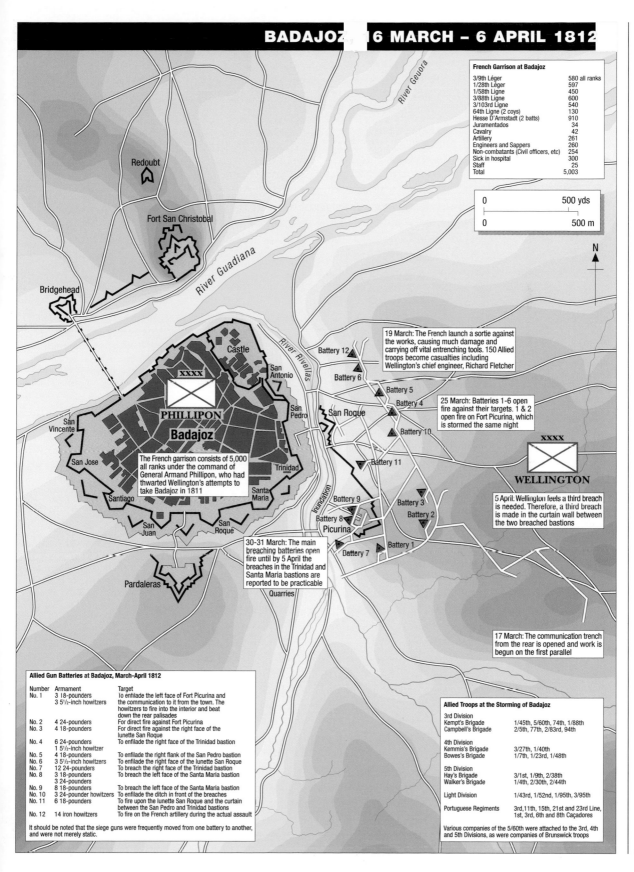

French Garrison at Badajoz

3/9th Léger	580 all ranks
1/28th Léger	597
1/58th Ligne	450
3/88th Ligne	600
3/103rd Ligne	540
64th Ligne (2 coys)	130
Hesse D'Armstadt (2 batts)	910
Juramentados	34
Cavalry	42
Artillery	261
Engineers and Sappers	260
Non-combatants (Civil officers, etc)	254
Sick in hospital	300
Staff	25
Total	**5,003**

0		500 yds
0		500 m

N

19 March: The French launch a sortie against the works, causing much damage and carrying off vital entrenching tools. 150 Allied troops become casualties including Wellington's chief engineer, Richard Fletcher

25 March: Batteries 1-6 open fire against their targets. 1 & 2 open fire on Fort Picurina, which is stormed the same night

XXXX
WELLINGTON

5 April. Wellington feels a third breach is needed. Therefore, a third breach is made in the curtain wall between the two breached bastions

XXXX
PHILLIPON

Badajoz

The French garrison consists of 5,000 all ranks under the command of General Armand Phillipon, who had thwarted Wellington's attempts to take Badajoz in 1811

30-31 March: The main breaching batteries open fire until by 5 April the breaches in the Trinidad and Santa Maria bastions are reported to be practicable

17 March: The communication trench from the rear is opened and work is begun on the first parallel

Redoubt

Fort San Christobal

Bridgehead

River Guadiana

River Geuora

Castle

San Antonio

San Pedro

San Roque

Battery 12

Battery 6

Battery 5

Battery 4

Battery 10

Battery 11

Battery 9

Battery 3

Battery 8

Battery 2

Battery 1

Battery 7

Picurina

Trinidad

Santa Maria

San Vincente

San Jose

Santiago

San Juan

San Roque

Pardaleras

Quarries

Inundation

River Rivellas

Allied Gun Batteries at Badajoz, March-April 1812

Number	Armament	Target
No. 1	3 18-pounders 3 5½-inch howitzers	To enfilade the left face of Fort Picurina and the communication to it from the town. The howitzers to fire into the interior and beat down the rear palisades
No. 2	4 24-pounders	For direct fire against Fort Picurina
No. 3	4 18-pounders	For direct fire against the right face of the lunette San Roque
No. 4	6 24-pounders 1 5½-inch howitzer	To enfilade the right face of the Trinidad bastion
No. 5	4 18-pounders	To enfilade the right flank of the San Pedro bastion
No. 6	3 5½-pounder howitzers	To enfilade the right face of the lunette San Roque
No. 7	12 24-pounders	To breach the right face of the Trinidad bastion
No. 8	3 18-pounders 3 24-pounders	To breach the left face of the Santa Maria bastion
No. 9	8 18-pounders	To breach the left face of the Santa Maria bastion
No. 10	3 24-pounder howitzers	To enfilade the ditch in front of the breaches
No. 11	6 18-pounders	To fire upon the lunette San Roque and the curtain between the San Pedro and Trinidad bastions
No. 12	14 iron howitzers	To fire on the French artillery during the actual assault

It should be noted that the siege guns were frequently moved from one battery to another, and were not merely static.

Allied Troops at the Storming of Badajoz

3rd Division
Kempt's Brigade	1/45th, 5/60th, 74th, 1/88th
Campbell's Brigade	2/5th, 77th, 2/83rd, 94th

4th Division
Kemmis's Brigade	3/27th, 1/40th
Bowes's Brigade	1/7th, 1/23rd, 1/48th

5th Division
Hay's Brigade	3/1st, 1/9th, 2/38th
Walker's Brigade	1/4th, 2/30th, 2/44th

Light Division	1/43rd, 1/52nd, 1/95th, 3/95th
Portuguese Regiments	3rd,11th, 15th, 21st and 23rd Line, 1st, 3rd, 6th and 8th Caçadores

Various companies of the 5/60th were attached to the 3rd, 4th and 5th Divisions, as were companies of Brunswick troops

3 had been thrown up only towards the end of 1811 but by the time of the third siege was formed to its proper shape. The ravelins of bastions 1, 2, 3 and 4 were begun in February 1812, when Phillipon received the first reports of the possibility of a renewed siege. Given the shortage of time the defenders did a remarkable job, working long and hard to raise the height of the ravelins to about three feet above the glacis. A lunette of 6 feet deep and as many wide was started in the ditch from bastions 1 to 3, but in spite of this these three bastions were considered by the French to be the weakest point in the defences and suspected that it would be here that Wellington would choose to make his breaches. One very significant innovation was the building of a dam with sluices in the ditch of the left face of the lunette San Roque. This prevented the waters

Another view of Badajoz, published by Edward Orme in 1812. British troops march towards the bridge while the familiar skyline of the town stands in the background.

of the Rivellas from flowing into the Guadiana and thus formed a false lake or inundation, which would cramp Wellington's assaulting columns and cause them serious problems.

Apart from the actual fortifications, Phillipon's men worked hard at opening up new embrasures for their guns as well as constructing traverses to guard against enfilade. They also set about making the dreaded chevaux-de-frises, planks of wood bristling with sharp sword blades, which would be hauled into position immediately prior to the Allied assault. The central part of the defence was the castle. It was not really a castle in the traditional sense of the word, but merely an enclosure surrounded by walls varying from between 19 to 46 feet high. The garrison's main powder magazine was stored here as were most of the provisions. In the event of Wellington's men gaining the breaches, Phillipon intended to retreat to within the castle and hold it as a place of final defence. Gun batteries were overhauled and new ones constructed, whilst miners worked round the clock at the foot of the walls, hacking away at their rocky base to increase the depth of the ditch. The walls were high enough on their own, but, given the fact that they stood on top of a hill high above the Guadiana, they formed a very strong position. Indeed, the castle enclosure was considered to be the strongest and most secure part of the defences.

With Badajoz having been encircled by Wellington's men, his engineers set about the task of deciding where the breaches would be made in the walls. During the failed sieges in May and June 1811, the Allies had chosen the castle and the San Christobal as the points of attack. This would not be repeated, however, and after careful consideration by Richard Fletcher, in consultation with both his colleagues and with Wellington, it was decided that the main focus for the attack should be the south-east front of the town at bastions 6 and 7, the Santa Maria and the Trinidad bastions. The French had strengthened the works along the south and south-west of the town, perhaps under the impression that, as they had attacked here in 1811, so Wellington would chose to do likewise. They were wrong, however, and the Santa Maria and Trinidad bastions, along with the curtain wall

between them, were chosen as the site for the breaches. Naturally, this entailed the capturing of Fort Picurina, the outwork that protected this front from attack.

Before Wellington's engineers could contemplate any of the above, however, the business of 'breaking ground', that is beginning the first parallel, had to be done. On the night of 17 March some 1,800 workmen, with a further 2,000 men acting as the covering party, assembled to begin digging the first parallel but it was so wet and windy that it took three hours for work to begin. The actual digging was an anxious time for the workmen as they were digging just 160 yards from Fort Picurina and it was just as well that the stormy conditions drowned the noise of both pick and shovel. By daylight on 18 March, a parallel of around 600 yards, 3 feet deep and $3\frac{1}{2}$ feet wide, had been dug along with a communication trench to the rear measuring 4,000 feet. All in all, it was a fairly good night's work although daylight exposed the workers to the full firepower of the French troops in the fort, who opened fire with musketry and the occasional round shot which continued most of the day. During the night of 18 March the parallel was extended by a further 450 yards in spite of the heavy rain.

The work continued unabated on 19 March when suddenly the working parties were attacked by about 1,500 French infantry supported by 40 cavalry who had filed out of the town unseen from the lunette San Roque to Fort Picurina. The French troops quickly filled the trenches, driving off the working parties, which were caught completely by surprise. Sections of the parallel were filled in and 200 valuable entrenching tools carried off. In fact, Phillipon had offered bounties for each tool brought away by his men. French dragoons rode in and out of the works, cutting down all those who opposed them and eventually the French managed to penetrate some 100 yards into the rear of the parallel before they were finally brought to book by the working parties and

British infantry constructing a bridge over the Guadiana prior to the siege in 1811. The scene would have been repeated in March 1812, when both a pontoon bridge and a 'flying' bridge were constructed over the Guadiana. From a picture by Browne.

by the guard, who were rallied by some officers. The British troops then turned upon the French, who were forced out of the parallel and driven back to the town, but not before they had done considerable damage to the works. During the sortie Sir Richard Fletcher, trying desperately to prevent the French from carrying off the tools, was badly wounded when he was struck in the groin by a musket ball, which drove a silver dollar an inch into the wound. It probably saved his life and although he was effectively sidelined throughout the rest of the siege, Wellington would consult with him daily on the siege's progress.

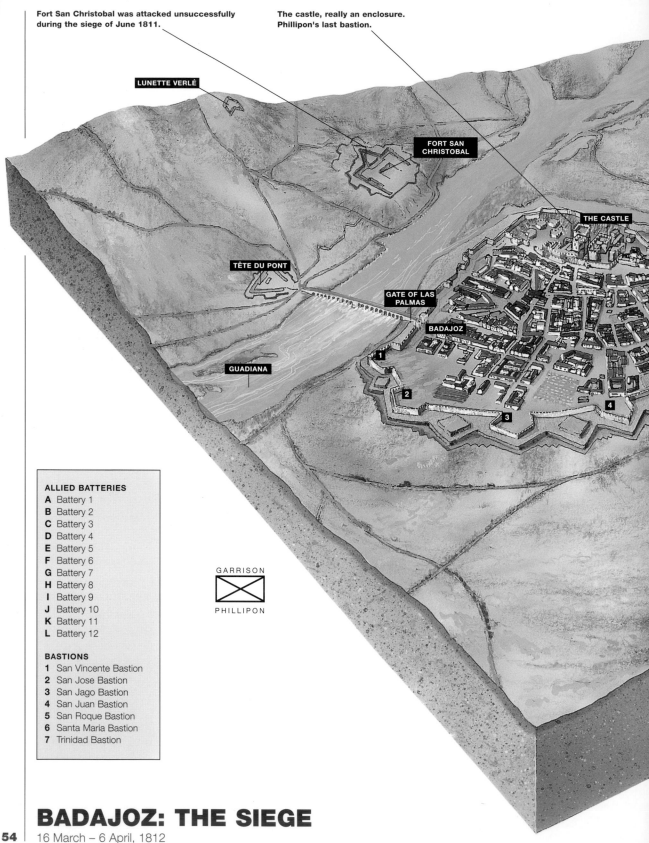

Fort San Christobal was attacked unsuccessfully during the siege of June 1811.

The castle, really an enclosure. Phillipon's last bastion.

LUNETTE VERLÉ

FORT SAN CHRISTOBAL

THE CASTLE

TÊTE DU PONT

GATE OF LAS PALMAS

BADAJOZ

GUADIANA

ALLIED BATTERIES
A Battery 1
B Battery 2
C Battery 3
D Battery 4
E Battery 5
F Battery 6
G Battery 7
H Battery 8
I Battery 9
J Battery 10
K Battery 11
L Battery 12

BASTIONS
1 San Vincente Bastion
2 San Jose Bastion
3 San Jago Bastion
4 San Juan Bastion
5 San Roque Bastion
6 Santa Maria Bastion
7 Trinidad Bastion

GARRISON

PHILLIPON

BADAJOZ: THE SIEGE

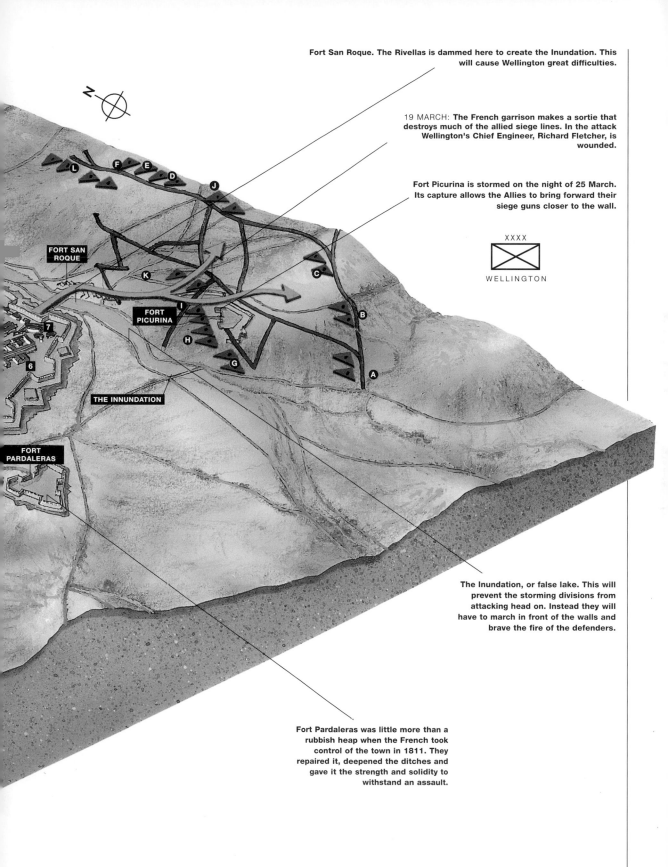

Fort San Roque. The Rivellas is dammed here to create the Inundation. This will cause Wellington great difficulties.

19 MARCH: The French garrison makes a sortie that destroys much of the allied siege lines. In the attack Wellington's Chief Engineer, Richard Fletcher, is wounded.

Fort Picurina is stormed on the night of 25 March. Its capture allows the Allies to bring forward their siege guns closer to the wall.

XXXX

WELLINGTON

The Inundation, or false lake. This will prevent the storming divisions from attacking head on. Instead they will have to march in front of the walls and brave the fire of the defenders.

Fort Pardaleras was little more than a rubbish heap when the French took control of the town in 1811. They repaired it, deepened the ditches and gave it the strength and solidity to withstand an assault.

FORT SAN ROQUE

FORT PICURINA

THE INNUNDATION

FORT PARDALERAS

N

L F E D J K I C B H G A 7 6

This very accurate painting by Captain T. St. Clair shows the Allied working parties digging the first parallel before Badajoz. As with all of St Clair's paintings – he was an eye-witness, a British officer serving with the Portuguese army – the picture bristles with detail. The puffs of smoke from the middle distance mark the location of Fort Picurina, while to the left centre, on a slight rise, can be seen British riflemen returning the fort's fire. A team of oxen has brought forward one of the huge 24-pounder guns, while workmen hack away with pick and shovel. This is the view that the majority of Wellington's men had of Badajoz throughout the siege, with the French flag taunting them from the tower in the castle, right.

The work pressed on with the parallels being lengthened and batteries constructed, but as the work progressed so the weather worsened. One of the main consequences of the heavy rain was the fact that the earth that was dug out of the parallel refused to pile up but simply turned to liquid mud. This meant that there was little protection for the workmen. Under normal circumstances, the spoil would provide a sort of rampart capable of absorbing enemy shot but in the torrential rain in the trenches before Badajoz this became impossible. It was a situation that would become so familiar to the descendants of Wellington's army just over one hundred years later. On 22 March the rain fell in torrents, moving Jones to call it, 'one of the heaviest showers imaginable'. So heavy was it, in fact, that the pontoon bridge across the Guadiana was carried away by the river and it became doubtful whether it would be possible to get supplies and ammunition across. So serious was the problem that there was the distinct possibility of the siege being abandoned. The following day, however, the rain stopped and the pontoon bridge restored and work continued. At 3pm the rain started to fall again and continued for the next four hours, saturating the earth and flooding the trenches. The earth lost all its consistency and simply slithered back into the trenches as fast as it was dug out. This thoroughly miserable situation meant that the guns could not be got forward into the batteries and valuable time was lost.

On the night of 24 March the weather was good enough to allow the batteries to be armed and at 11am on 25 March the guns opened up aginst Fort Picurina, the garrison replying with its own artillery. The guns pounded away throughout the day with the fort's defences crumbling at every shot until by nightfall it was decided to attack the place. The orders for the assault were given by Major-General Kempt, who commanded in the

trenches that day. The attack would be made by 500 men of the 3rd and Light Divisions, formed into three detatchments; the right, consisting of 200 men under Major Shaw of the 74th, the centre, consisting of 100 men under Captain Powis of the 83rd and the left, 200 men under Major Rudd of the 77th. The detatchments would be guided by Royal Engineers along with carpenters and miners armed with axes, crow-bars and ladders, to break in the palisades. The garrison of the fort numbered 200 under the command of Colonel Gaspard Thierry, who had ordered 200 extra muskets to be placed along the ramparts in order that his men could fire several pieces.

The attack was scheduled for 9pm and at the appointed hour the attacking troops duly sprang from their trenches and moved forward towards the glacis. It was inevitable that they would be detected by the French, who held their fire until their assailants reached the glacis. Then, all at once, the silent, black mass of the fort became alive with fire as Thierry's men opened up, the first volleys of musketry bringing down at least 100 British troops before they had even reached the ditch. The ladders were then placed in the ditch but many were found to be too short, whilst the thick palisades presented an impenetrable barrier. Sappers and miners alike hacked at them to force an entrance, whilst all around them shells and grenades exploded in the ditch. The guns of the garrison in Badajoz opened up also as the British troops struggled to gain the ramparts of the fort. At length Captain Oates of the 88th noticed that, although the ladders were too short they were, nevertheless, long enough to span the

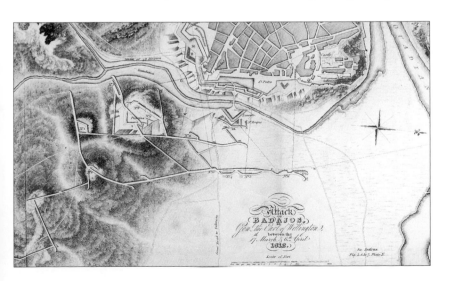

'The Attack of Badajoz by Gen. the Earl of Wellington'. The plan of the castle, breaches and Fort Picurina, as it appeared in the 1st Edition of Jones' *Journal of the Sieges in Spain*.

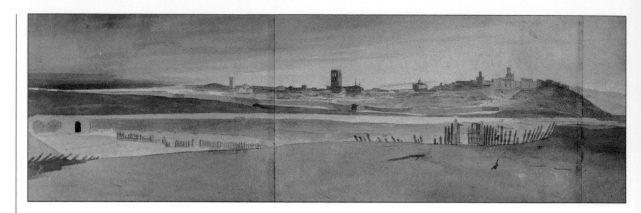

ABOVE **A view of Badajoz, as seen from Fort Picurina just after the capture of the latter. Away to the right can be seen the castle enclosure while the Inundation can clearly be identified as the long, light-coloured area running across the picture in the centre. The area of the breaches can be seen in the dead centre of this watercolour, which was painted by Captain C. G. Elliscombe, Royal Engineers.**

RIGHT **The remaining section of Fort Picurina today. This very thick section of wall was once part of the left or western flank of the fort. The fort was stormed on the night of 25 March and breaching batteries constructed in it the following day. Just visible on the left skyline is a crane, which marks the location of the curtain wall between the Santa Maria and Trinidad bastions. The Spaniards have evidently found it very difficult to demolish the fort, its thick, solid walls still standing in what is now a children's playground.**

ditch and three ladders were quickly thrown across as a sort of bridge, across which his men dashed, forcing their way into the fort through a partially repaired embrasure. At the same time, Captain Powis' detachment broke into the fort at the salient angle and soon the British troops were bayoneting their way in and Fort Picurina was taken.

The capture of the fort did not come cheap, for it cost Wellington 4 officers and 50 men killed, and 15 officers and 250 men wounded. The French lost 130 officers and men killed and wounded, whilst a further 60, including Thierry, were taken prisoner. Only one officer and 30 men managed to make it back to the town.

Phillipon did his best to prevent the Allies from entering the fort and turned his guns upon it. The barrage laid down on the fort was so heavy, in fact, that it was not until the evening of 26 March that a secure lodgement was made in the fort. During the night of 26–27 March the engineers began to trace out the ground for the batteries to be used to breach the bastions in Badajoz. No. 7 battery consisted of twelve 24-pounders, which were to breach the right face of the Trinidad bastion, while no. 9 battery consisted of eight 18-pounders, which were to breach the left face of the Santa Maria bastion. No. 10 battery, three 24-pounder iron howitzers, was to enfilade the ditch in front of the breaches to prevent the French from clearing away the debris there and to prevent them placing any obstacles.

A view of Badajoz from the remains of Fort Picurina. Batteries 8 and 9 were sited in the foreground on the football pitch, with no. 8 on the left and no. 9 on the right. The site of the curtain wall between the Santa Maria and Trinidad bastions lies in front of the block of flats to the left of centre above which can be seen a crane. The distance from Fort Picurina to the curtain wall is precisely 570 yards. This photo should be compared with the watercolour done by Captain Elliscombe of the Royal Engineers, which is shown opposite.

The work continued throughout the next few days until finally, on 30 March, the eight 18-pounders in battery no. 9 opened fire against the left flank of the Santa Maria bastion. Morale was certainly lifted by the sight of these mighty guns as they began to pound the wall, but when the smoke cleared after the first few shots there appeared to be little damage done. In fact, there was more damage inflicted on the besiegers when the magazine intended for use by battery no. 9 accidentally blew up after an accident, killing four artillerymen and wounding several others. Fortunately, more ammunition was brought over and the guns continued their work. The following day the twelve 24-pounders in battery no. 7 opened fire on the right face of the Trinidad bastion, but despite an almost continual bombardment little damage was done to the walls. The Allied artillery would not be denied, however, and soon the guns began to take their effect. By the evening of 1 April large areas of earth could clearly be seen in the face of the Trinidad bastion as it began to crumble, whilst the Santa Maria bastion also showed signs of damage.

During the next few days Wellington's gunners fired away with increased vigour, each shot bringing down both masonry and earth until by 5 April the breaches were reported as being as practicable as they could be. The fact was not lost on either Phillipon or his chief engineer, Lamare, who recorded seeing a long train of wagons loaded with scaling ladders and, 'all the preparations which announced an approaching assault'. Indeed, as Wellington's gunners worked tirelessly to enlarge the breaches so Phillipon's men were equally relentless in their efforts to clear the ditch of debris and to carry out as much repair work as the enemy artillery fire would allow. Retrenchments were dug behind the breaches and guns laid in position to sweep the breaches in the event of the Allies passing through. Meanwhile, all of the terrible defensive devices, such as the chevaux-de-frises, were being carefully assembled, ready to be placed in position the minute Wellington's men delivered the assault. It was pointless trying to block the breaches until the hour of the assault as the siege guns would simply blast them away.

The breaches being reported practicable, Wellington took himself off to the trenches to make a personal inspection. There is little doubt that Wellington knew the impending assault would cost the lives of hundreds of his men. The breaches yawned wide before him and the great prize of the fortress of Badajoz now lay within his grasp. And yet even now, a degree of self-doubt seems to have risen within him. Possibly the unhappy memories of the assault on Fort San Christobal the previous year still

ABOVE **Another view of Badajoz, this time from the south-west. The Roman bridge can be seen away to the left, while Fort San Christobal is visible on the hill about a third of the way in from the left. Other familiar landmarks can also be seen, such as the castle, the cathedral and the peculiar round-roofed building which features in all paintings of the town, and which still stands today. From a water-colour by Captain G. C. Elliscombe, Royal Engineers.**

RIGHT **'The Defence of Badajoz'. This engraving by Philippoteaux depicts Phillipon's men vowing to defend Badajoz to the last. The officer on Phillipon's left holds an Imperial Eagle, although none are recorded as having been present in the town. Certainly none were taken by Wellington's men.**

lingered. Certainly, the recent memory of the assault on Ciudad Rodrigo was still fresh in his mind. There he had lost his finest commander of light troops, Robert Craufurd, as well as Henry Mackinnon and a host of other good officers and men. Just how many men would he lose this time? It is quite probable that Wellington wished to see Badajoz fall without assault, possibly through starvation, but the decision was made for him when he received news that Soult and his relieving force had reached Llerena, some 70 miles to the south, forcing Hill, with the covering force, to retire towards Talavera whilst Graham marched to join Wellington at Badajoz. It was now or never. Wellington, however, wary of the hot welcome which Phillipon was preparing for his men, still wanted his stormers to have as easy an entry as was humanly possible and, after inspecting the breaches with his engineers, decided to cancel the assault – which had been planned for the night of 5 April – in order to make a new breach in the curtain wall between the Santa Maria and Trinidad bastions. Accordingly, all the breaching batteries were brought to bear against the curtain wall, opening fire on 6 April. To their great credit, Wellington's gunners succeeded in making a breach in the wall close to the Trinidad bastion. Once again Wellington inspected the breaches and decided that the assault would be delivered that same night.

But if Wellington entertained any doubts as to the outcome of the attack his men certainly did not. In fact, they were positively itching to get up the walls and into the breaches. To say they were straining at the leash is putting it mildly. John Kincaid, that famous raconteur of the 95th, wrote, 'In proportion as the grand crisis approached, the anxiety of the soldiers increased, not on any account of any doubt or dread as to the result, but for fear that the place may be surrendered without standing an assault, for, singular as it may appear, although there was a certainty of about one man out of every three being knocked down, there were perhaps not three men in the three divisions who would not rather have braved all the chances than receive it tamely from the hands of the enemy. So great was the rage for passports into eternity, in any battalion, on that occassion, that even the officers' servants insisted on taking their place in the ranks, and I was obliged to leave my baggage in charge of a man who had been wounded some days before'. Perhaps the most chilling observation was made by William Grattan, of the 88th, who wrote, 'The spirits of the soldiers, which no fatigues could dampen, rose to a frightful height … there was a certain something in their bearing … every fine feeling vanished and plunder and revenge took their place … In a word, the capture of Badajoz had long been their idol; many causes led to their wish on their part; the two previous unsuccessful sieges, and the failure of the attack against San Christobal in the latter; but above all, the well known hostility of its inhabitants to the British army, and perhaps might be added, a desire for plunder which the sacking of Rodrigo had given them a taste for. Badajoz was, therefore, denounced as a place to be made example of; and most unquestionably no city, Jerusalem exempted, was ever more strictly visited to the letter than was this ill-fated town'. Sadly for the unfortunate inhabitants of Badajoz, Grattan's words proved to be all too true.

Wellington's orders for the assault, which were written down prior to the creation of the third breach, ran to 27 paragraphs, with certain notes and amendments added afterwards. Basically, Picton's 3rd Division was to move forward from the first parallel shortly before 10pm. It was to cross the Rivellas and take the castle by escalade. The 4th Division, under Colville, was to leave behind a covering party in the trenches, before moving off to storm the breach in the Trinidad bastion. Barnard's Light Division was to storm the Santa Maria breach. Barnard was also to place 100 men in the quarries near the covered way of the Santa Maria bastion to keep down the fire of the defenders placed there. Firing parties would also be placed along the glacis to keep down the enemy's fire whilst storming parties rushed the breaches. The advance parties of each storming division would consist of 500 men, carrying twelve ladders, and would be preceded by the men of the Forlorn Hope who were to carry large sacks of grass which were to be thrown into the ditches to break the fall of the troops jumping into it. Leith meanwhile was to make a false attack with the 5th Division on Fort Pardaleras and, if a favourable opportunity arose, they were to make an attempt to take the San Vincente bastion by escalade. Elsewhere, Major Wilson of the 48th was to lead a party against the

One of the pages of Wellington's handwritten orders for the assault on Badajoz. Note how he has added an amendment to them in the top right corner. Here, it says 'General Colville will observe that a part of the advance of the 4th Division must be allotted to storm the new Breach in the curtain'. This is a reference to the breach made in the curtain between the Santa Maria and Trinidad bastions. The orders were originally written down prior to the third breach having been made, hence the addition of this clause.

The Forlorn Hope prepares to move forward at Badajoz on 6 April 1812. This romantic version even has two men of the Household Cavalry preparing to go forward.

lunette San Roque whilst General Power's Portuguese brigade was to make a false attack on Fort San Christobal.

The hour for the assault was originally set for 7.30pm but it proved impossible for Wellington's men to complete their preparations. Therefore, the attack was put back until 10pm, giving the French defenders a valuable $2^1/_2$ hours in which to shore up and improve their defences. The delay proved to be a costly one for Wellington's men because Phillipon and his garrison set about blocking the breaches with all sorts of simple but very deadly obstacles. At the foot of the counterscarp, Phillipon had dug a ditch which raised its height to 16 feet. Wellington had planned to form his men in this ditch but the garrison, unseen by the besiegers, had filled it with water which would give the stormers a great deal of trouble. In the breaches themselves were placed all sorts of obstacles including the savage chevaux-de-frises, made from razor-sharp cavalry sabres; fascines, sandbags and woolpacks replaced fallen ramparts and the slopes of the breaches were covered with planks of wood, studded with 12-inch spikes and chained to the ground. Explosives were taken from the artillery stores and powder barrels were placed, ready to be rolled down into the ditches to explode amongst the crowded ranks of stormers when they attacked. Finally, at the foot of the counterscarp, immediately in front of the breaches, were arranged sixty 14-inch shells, at about four yards apart, in a circle, which were covered with earth, whilst powder hoses, placed between tubes, were designed to act as fuses. These mines would cause havoc amongst the densely packed ranks of the stormers as soon as they entered the ditches. All in all, Badajoz bristled with all manner of defensive devices. If Wellington was going to take Badajoz, Phillipon was going to make him pay in the blood of his best troops.

THE ASSAULT

The night of 6 April 1812 was destined to be one of the greatest nights in the history of the British army. It was certainly the most momentous night of the Peninsular War for Wellington's men. Before them lay the fortress of Badajoz, a prize which had eluded them on two previous occasions. This time they were determined to make it 'third time lucky'. The night itself was extremely dark, an eerie mist rose from the nearby river Guadiana, and the silence was broken only by the incessant croaking of the frogs in that river and in the Rivellas. The artillery fire of the past couple of weeks 'now ceased as if by mutual consent, and a deathlike silence of nearly an hour preceded the awful scene of carnage'. This silence, however, was soon to be shattered as the violent events of the night unfolded.

It is difficult to imagine the emotions amongst Wellington's men as they lay waiting in the trenches before Badajoz. We know that a sense of

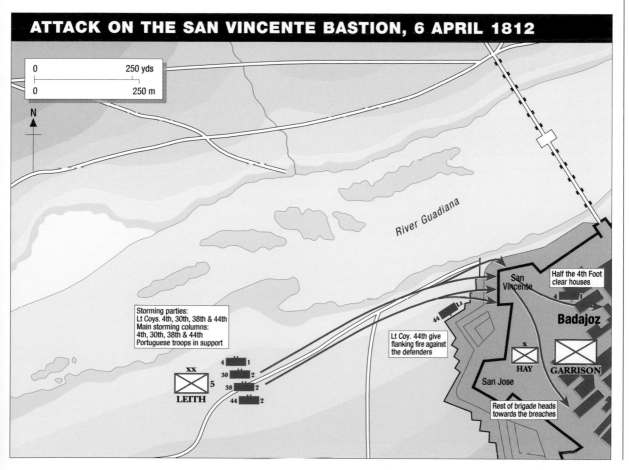

ATTACK ON THE SAN VINCENTE BASTION, 6 APRIL 1812

0 ___ 250 yds
0 ___ 250 m

N

River Guadiana

Storming parties:
Lt Coys. 4th, 30th, 38th & 44th
Main storming columns:
4th, 30th, 38th & 44th
Portuguese troops in support

Lt Coy. 44th give
flanking fire against
the defenders

San
Vincente

Half the 4th Foot
clear houses

Badajoz

44

XX

LEITH

4   1
30   2
38   2
44   2

5

X
HAY

GARRISON

San Jose

Rest of brigade heads
towards the breaches

A contemporary print depicting the storming of Badajoz, 6 April 1812. Unlike the two prints showing the assault on Ciudad Rodrigo, this one is fairly accurate. On the right can be seen the 3rd Division scaling the walls of the castle, while in the centre the 4th and Light Divisions can be seen attacking the three breaches.

foreboding had descended upon their camp as they became focused on the task ahead of them. Many wrote letters and exchanged wills, some merely sat in silent reflection, whilst others no doubt considered how they intended to enjoy themselves once they were inside the town. The men had been allowed to discard their knapsacks, their shirts were unbuttoned and many were barefoot and had their trousers tucked in at the knees. They were barely recognisable as British soldiers but, as Napier wrote, 'their self-confidence … gave them the appearance of what they, in reality, were – an invincible host'.

At about 9.30pm, the storming columns, preceded by the Forlorn Hope, began to move forward to their jumping-off stations. They could hear the French sentries calling out 'Tout va bien', on the ramparts. Not for long, they probably thought and, indeed, at twenty minutes to ten, Major Wilson of the 48th led his 300 men forward to attack the San Roque. The rattling of musketry broke the silence of the night, ladders were placed in the ditch and soon the fort was taken with very little resistance. Finally, as the church bells in the town tolled the hour, the stormers moved off into the darkness to begin the main assault.

The breaches in the Santa Maria and Trinidad bastions, and in the curtain wall between them, were the objective of the 4th and Light Divisions, who made their way forward on the left bank of the Inundation. As soon as they reached the edge of the glacis the men carrying grassbags threw them into the ditch whilst others placed ladders in it to facilitate the men's descent. Tragically, a number of men jumped into that part of the ditch which was filled with water and many were drowned before the mistake was realised. The ditch quickly filled up with a seething mass of British and Portuguese soldiers whilst the Forlorn Hope struggled to the top of the breach in the Trinidad bastion. Then, out of the night sky, came a lighted carcass, thrown from the ramparts, and just as suddenly the whole scene was illuminated as the defenders opened up with a blaze of musketry and artillery fire, sweeping away the Forlorn Hope in an instant. Grenades and other combustibles were

The walls of the castle at Badajoz. It was along here, at the ditch which once ran along the foot of these walls, that Picton's 3rd Division placed its ladders before scaling the walls in the face of a very determined French resistance. This section was attacked by Campbell's brigade, while Kempt attacked the walls further to the left of this photo.

'Badajoz taken by Storm on the 6th of April 1812 by the Allied Army under Lord Wellington'. This engraving depicts the assault on the breaches. The men are wearing the correct uniforms, the plate having been done in 1813, before the 1812-pattern shakos had become general issue.

simply tossed into the ditch to explode amongst the stormers. It was all too easy for the French, who now detonated one of the mines which they had placed beneath the breach. Scores of men were cast into the night sky by the violence of the explosion whilst on the edge of the glacis the men of the 4th and Light Divisions watched in awe, 'amazed by the terrific sight', as their comrades were blown apart in front of them.

The story of the violent, volcanic struggle at the breaches can only really be told by the men who were there and space precludes including their own accounts here. It will suffice to say that Wellington's men had never before faced anything like the inferno into which they now poured, to death, destruction and to glory. They had never been asked

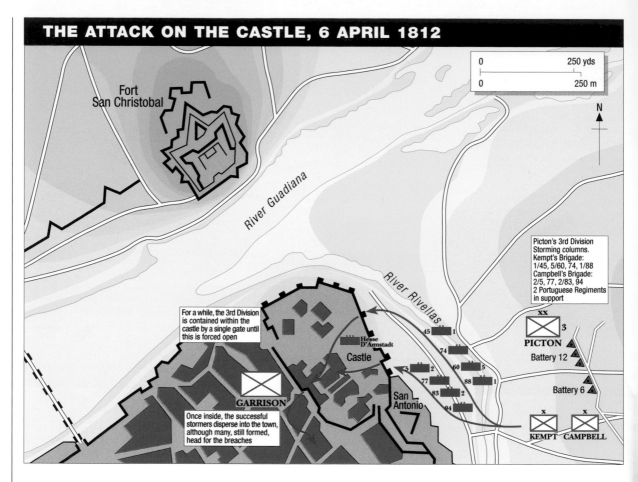

0   250 yds

0   250 m

Fort San Christobal

River Guadiana

River Rivellas

Picton's 3rd Division
Storming columns.
Kempt's Brigade:
1/45, 5/60, 74, 1/88
Campbell's Brigade:
2/5, 77, 2/83, 94
2 Portuguese Regiments
in support

XX   3

PICTON   Battery 12

Battery 6

For a while, the 3rd Division is contained within the castle by a single gate until this is forced open

Hesse D'Amstadt

Castle

GARRISON

Once inside, the successful stormers disperse into the town, although many, still formed, head for the breaches

San Antonio

x   x

KEMPT   CAMPBELL

to do anything like it before, nor would they ever again. Men were dashed to atoms by the explosions, shot by musket or crushed by rocks and logs hurled down by the defenders. The attackers could not pass the terrible chevaux-de-frises that blocked the breaches and all those who attempted to pass were simply shot or bayoneted. One British officer tried to crawl under it but he was found the next morning with his brains beaten out. The chaos was incredible as both divisions became inextricably mixed, growing ever more desperate to get into the town. In the confusion, the ravelin protecting the curtain wall between the breaches was mistaken for a breach, due mainly to its ruined state. In the darkness and confusion the men thought it must be a breach and up they went, only to be swept away by a few rounds of grape shot from the French guns. It was sheer slaughter. Indeed, such was the fire from the defenders that one survivor wrote that it was 'unlike anything hitherto witnessed by the oldest soldier'. Added to all the musketry and the fire and glare of the explosions was the cheering from both sides, the cries of the wounded and dying and the exultant battle cries of the French defenders, who taunted their assailants with shouts of, 'why don't you come into Badajoz?' Altogether, it is said that Wellington's men made forty separate attacks on the breaches, only to be hurled back forty times, leaving an ever-increasing pile of dead and dying men in the ditches. Midnight came and went and with not a single British or Portuguese soldier having managed to pass through the breaches alive and with

RIGHT **The site of the breach in the Trinidad bastion, Badajoz. Like that in the Santa Maria bastion, the year '1812' was once picked out in cannonballs, which have now gone. The holes can still be seen, however, at the top of this photo.**

BELOW, RIGHT **Another view of the site of the breach in the Trinidad bastion. In 1812 the spot from which this photo was taken was the ditch, a mass of British and Portuguese soldiers, most of whom would have been either killed or wounded. This spot is one of the most awesome places in the Peninsula, and many a good man was either buried beneath the walls or interred within them afterwards.**

Lieutenant-Colonel Henry Ridge of the 5th Foot. Ridge is traditionally accepted as being the first man to get inside Badajoz, having scaled one of the ladders with his men protecting his head with their bayonets and swords. Sadly, Ridge was among the many Allied dead, being shot soon after he entered the castle.

almost 2,000 casualties already sustained in this small, bloody area, the men began to despair of ever getting inside Badajoz.

Having spent the past two weeks creating breaches in the walls of Badajoz, it is ironic that the two assaults by escalade were to decide the fate of the town. Picton's 3rd Division had crossed the Rivellas at around 10pm and even as the men began to pick their way up the slopes towards the castle walls, the main attacks on the breaches got under way. Indeed, so anxious was Picton to get forward that, upon hearing the sounds of musketry and explosions away to his left, he threatened to cut down the guide, Lieutenant MacCarthy, who he feared had lost the way. Fortunately for MacCarthy the 3rd Division had taken the correct route, a fact borne out by the heavy fire opened upon it as the men neared the walls.

The men of the 3rd Division had no breach to pass but they did have some very high walls to escalade, walls which were lined with French

ABOVE **An aerial view, taken in 1914, of Badajoz's western defences. The San Vincente bastion (3) was scaled by Leith's 5th Division, while the San Jose (2) and Santiago (1) bastions are also marked. (4) marks the spot where the French breached the walls during their siege in 1811. Today, the bastions remain, albeit a little scruffy, as do sections of the walls, although the glacis has been completely built over.**

LEFT **The 5th Division scaling the walls of the San Vincente bastion at Badajoz, 6 April 1812. Note the men standing on each other's shoulders to compensate for the short ladders.**

RIGHT **'The Light Division at the taking of Badajoz, April 6th 1812', from a picture by Wollen. Men, debris and discarded ladders already litter the ditch as the men of the Light Division descend into it to attack the breaches. This picture has a good deal of accuracy and a lot of atmosphere.**

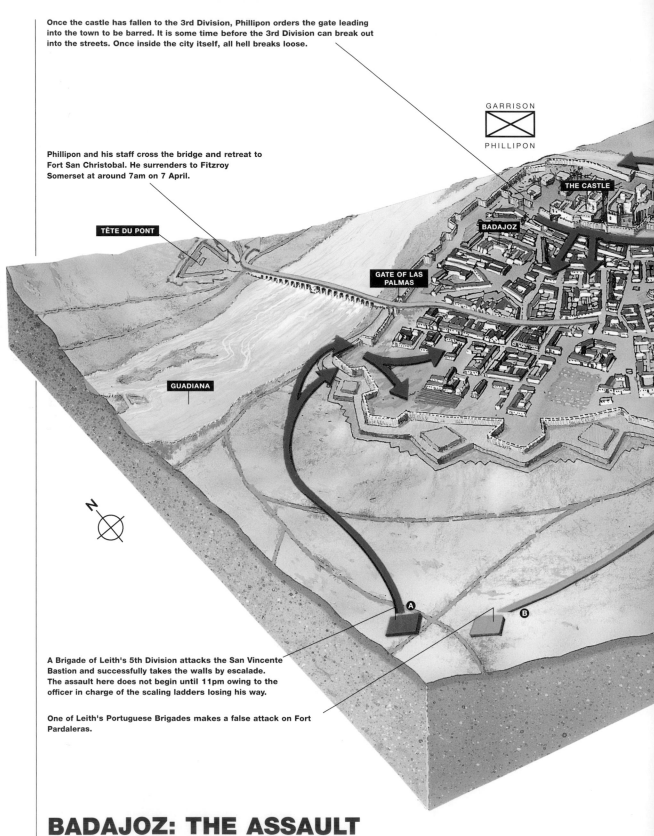

Once the castle has fallen to the 3rd Division, Phillipon orders the gate leading into the town to be barred. It is some time before the 3rd Division can break out into the streets. Once inside the city itself, all hell breaks loose.

GARRISON

PHILLIPON

Phillipon and his staff cross the bridge and retreat to Fort San Christobal. He surrenders to Fitzroy Somerset at around 7am on 7 April.

THE CASTLE

BADAJOZ

TÊTE DU PONT

GATE OF LAS PALMAS

GUADIANA

A

B

N

A Brigade of Leith's 5th Division attacks the San Vincente Bastion and successfully takes the walls by escalade. The assault here does not begin until 11pm owing to the officer in charge of the scaling ladders losing his way.

One of Leith's Portuguese Brigades makes a false attack on Fort Pardaleras.

BADAJOZ: THE ASSAULT
The night of 6–7 April, 1812

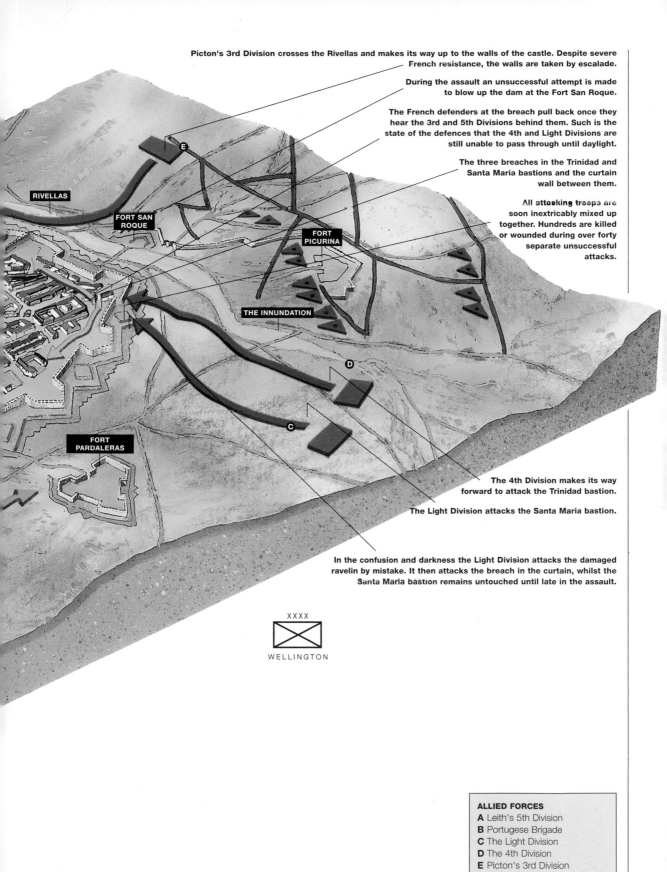

Picton's 3rd Division crosses the Rivellas and makes its way up to the walls of the castle. Despite severe French resistance, the walls are taken by escalade.

During the assault an unsuccessful attempt is made to blow up the dam at the Fort San Roque.

The French defenders at the breach pull back once they hear the 3rd and 5th Divisions behind them. Such is the state of the defences that the 4th and Light Divisions are still unable to pass through until daylight.

The three breaches in the Trinidad and Santa Maria bastions and the curtain wall between them.

All attacking troops are soon inextricably mixed up together. Hundreds are killed or wounded during over forty separate unsuccessful attacks.

The 4th Division makes its way forward to attack the Trinidad bastion.

The Light Division attacks the Santa Maria bastion.

In the confusion and darkness the Light Division attacks the damaged ravelin by mistake. It then attacks the breach in the curtain, whilst the Santa Maria bastion remains untouched until late in the assault.

RIVELLAS

FORT SAN ROQUE

FORT PICURINA

THE INNUNDATION

FORT PARDALERAS

E

D

C

XXXX

WELLINGTON

ALLIED FORCES
A Leith's 5th Division
B Portugese Brigade
C The Light Division
D The 4th Division
E Picton's 3rd Division

OPPOSITE, TOP 'The Storming of the Castle of Badajoz' by Richard Caton Woodville. Probably the most famous and certainly the most atmospheric depiction of the storming on 6 April 1812. The bare-headed officer in the centre is almost certainly Henry Ridge of the 5th. Behind him, British troops mount their ladders in the face of heavy French resistance before they finally establish themselves on the ramparts.

OPPOSITE, BOTTOM This remarkable photo, taken in 1914, shows the area of the breaches as it would have appeared to Wellington a century before. The Trinidad bastion (2) and the Santa Maria bastion (3) can clearly be seen, as can the ravelin, which covers the curtain wall between them. It was this ravelin, damaged by artillery fire, which was attacked in error by the 4th and Light Divisions. The original course of the Rivellas stream is marked by the tree line in front of the breaches. Today, it has been canalised and runs further to the right of this photo, roughly where the track on the right is. The Inundation was created by the dam at the bridge over the Rivellas at the lunette San Roque, which can be seen between the San Pedro bastion (1) and the Trinidad bastion. It flooded the area on both sides of the tree line as far as the Santa Maria bastion before it flowed away from the breaches. It was in the area between (2) and (3) that most of the slaughter took place on the night of 6 April 1812.

RIGHT The same view in 1978. The Trinidad bastion (2) and Santa Maria bastion (3) can be seen, while a road runs through the curtain wall between them. The ravelin has long since gone, gardens and houses cover the old glacis and another road runs through the far side of the Trinidad bastion.

defenders, who found the business of defending them relatively easy. The dropping of a barrel of gunpowder or grenade was quite a simple but effective way of dealing with the men who now crowded around in despair in the ditch at the foot of the walls, whilst any men fortunate enough to reach the top of the walls became easy victims for the French, who just thrust their bayonets or swords into the faces of their would-be assailants. Or they simply shot them. In many cases the ladders proved to be too short, forcing the men to climb on to the shoulders of the men at the top of the ladders and, in some cases, on to their shoulders in turn. It was a strange operation which belonged more to the circus than the battlefield, as men balancing on each other's shoulders were tipped backwards by the French on to the bayonets of their comrades waiting below. Rocks, explosives and logs of wood were dropped down to crush the British troops at the foot of the walls and the situation became as desperate as that at the breaches. Even Picton was wounded, as was his successor, Kempt. It needed something very special and very extraordinary to break the deadlock, and that something was provided by Colonel Henry Ridge of the 5th Foot.

Despairing of the situation, which grew worse around him, Ridge grabbed a ladder and planted it at the walls further to the left of the main attack where the walls were slightly lower. Calling for his men to follow him, he began to climb up, the swords and bayonets of his men being held up to protect him. Soon, the ladder was crowded with others and it proved impossible for the French to push it away from the walls. Ridge pressed on until he reached the top of the wall and then, by some miracle, he found himself standing on the ramparts along with a grenadier officer, Canch, of the same regiment. Others followed behind them and suddenly Wellington's men were up on the castle ramparts. The tide of battle had turned.

The small group of British troops made a sort of bridgehead until others followed them up, furiously climbing on to the ramparts which had denied them for so long. One regiment which had been busy defending the castle walls was the crack German regiment the Hesse D'Armstadt Regiment, who were shown little mercy by the enraged British troops who now got their revenge. 'Few, very few of those who had assisted in raising the pile of dead that now nearly filled the ditch, were left to boast of their deeds', recorded one survivor in his chilling account of the fight. The 3rd Division now began to drop down from the ramparts into the castle enclosure, the place where Phillipon had hoped to make his final stand. Sadly, Henry Ridge was not among them, for he had been mortally wounded soon after he had formed his men for the

The attack on the castle of Badajoz by Picton's 3rd Division was only intended as a diversionary attack, whilst the main assault was carried out at the breaches. In the event it was Picton's assault, by escalade, which proved successful, along with Leith's attack, also by escalade, at the San Vincente bastion. It was an incredible achievement given the size of the walls, but was one that cost the division heavy casualties, including Picton himself who was wounded in the foot.

ABOVE, LEFT **The storming of the castle of Badajoz, after a drawing by Captain Marshman. This unusual drawing shows the 83rd Regiment locked in combat with the defenders of the castle. There is much wrong as regards uniform detail, but otherwise the artist has captured the ferocity of the fight at the top of the walls. Planks with sharp spikes can be seen, as the combatants set about each other with axes in savage hand-to-hand fighting.**

BELOW, LEFT **Richard Simkin's version of the storming of Badajoz. Once again, the uniforms may be incorrect but the spirit is captured very well, with breaking ladders, crowded ditches and tenacious defenders throwing down rocks upon the heads of their assailants.**

ABOVE, RIGHT **'The Storming of Badajoz' after a print by Dupray. Another Victorian version of the storming which shows British infantry inside the castle.**

BELOW, RIGHT **Shortly after 10pm on the night of 6 April 1812, this spot, now a very pleasant garden, was probably among the hottest and most dangerous places on earth. At the extreme left-hand edge of this photo stands what was the curtain wall, the site of the breach made on 6 April. In the foreground, marked by shadows, was where the ravelin once stood. The ravelin was so damaged that, in the darkness and confusion, it was attacked by mistake by the storming divisions, who thought it to be one of the breaches. On the right is the Trinidad bastion. The great breach was made in the left face of the bastion, that is to say, the face obscured by the trees on the right. The flank of the bastion upon which the sun is shining was not damaged. The fire from Wellington's guns would have come screaming in from right to left, to smash into the walls on the right.**

advance. His men followed, however, and before long the French were in full flight through the gate, which led into Badajoz itself, although they took care to lock it afterwards and thus deprived the British troops entry for a while.

Meanwhile, Picton's men consolidated their position in the castle enclosure. Sir Edward Pakenham, later a hero at Salamanca and the victim of an American sniper at New Orleans, was one of them. Ahead of him was a Lieutenant Macpherson, of the 45th, who had two broken ribs, having been shot at point blank range whilst trying to climb over the ramparts. Fortunately, a Spanish dollar had turned the musket ball, although the broken ribs made breathing difficult. Macpherson rushed to the top of the tower from where the French flag had flown throughout the siege, taunting Wellington's men as they laboured in the rain in the trenches. There he came across a French sentry, who was quickly knocked down and the French flag lowered. Finding no British flag at hand to run up the flagpole, Macpherson removed his jacket and ran that up instead.

Back at the breaches the attacks by the 4th and Light Divisions began to peter out, and Wellington was just in the act of ordering them to re-form and try again when a messenger arrived, announcing the success of Picton's Division at the castle. Wellington, who was visibly stunned by what he was seeing, suddenly shook himself from the despair in which he found himself and exclaimed, 'then the place is ours!' And indeed it was, for whilst the 3rd Division was pouring over into the castle, Leith's 5th Division had performed similar heroics at the San Vincente bastion. Once again they had endured the fire of the defenders but had managed to escalade the walls, which were somewhat lower than those at the castle, in the teeth of stiff resistance. Once over, the men poured into the town, although they were forced back at one point when the cry went up that a mine had been lit in front of them. It was a false alarm but it was enough to throw them back, the French pursuing and bayonetting scores of men as they fled in confusion. Leith, however, had formed a reserve, which advanced and drove back the French, at which point resistance in this quarter ended.

The 7th (Royal) Fusiliers at the storming of Badajoz, 6 April 1812. The regiment formed part of the 4th Division which, along with the Light Division, was hurled against the breaches for what some eye-witnesses estimated to be forty times. Each attack ended in the same result, bloody failure. The defences proved to be so effective that it proved difficult to pass them in daylight the next day after the town was taken.

The defenders at the breaches were by now quite comfortable having beaten off every attack the 4th and Light Divisions had thrown at them. However, what they had not expected was the sound of British bugles behind them, and when news of the fall of the castle reached them their resistance crumbled. Phillipon, too, was shocked by the news, which reached him whilst he waited with his staff in the Plaza San Juan. At first he could not believe the report, but when an dragoon officer came galloping into the plaza to confirm the news he knew Badajoz was as good as lost but, to his great credit, he still made an attempt to rescue the situation and ordered about forty dragoons to charge the Plaza de Las Palmas, where the 5th Division appeared to be concentrating. The charge proved unsuccessful, however, and, losing no time, Phillipon, with his staff and about forty cavalry, rode out through the Las Palmas gate, crossed the Roman bridge over the Guadiana and rode to Fort San Christobal. Here, at around 7am on 7 April , Phillipon surrendered to Lord Fitzroy Somerset. Badajoz was finally in Wellington's hands.

THE SACKING OF BADAJOZ

The capture of Badajoz by Wellington's men remains one of the greatest acheivements of the British army, although the events which followed were some of the most shameful and disgraceful. Even before Phillipon had surrendered to Fitzroy Somerset, British and Portuguese troops had begun their orgy of destruction as they poured into the streets of the town in search of plunder, drink and women. Like the actual assault, the only way to appreciate the horrors of the sacking are by reading the shocking accounts written by eye witnesses afterwards. It will suffice to say that a whole range of crimes were committed, from murder, rape, pillage, drunkeness and arson, to lesser crimes, most of which were inflicted upon the poor inhabitants. British officers trying to restore order were assaulted and, in some cases, shot by their own men. Every battalion had a hard core of criminals and it was around these that most of the bad deeds centred, with others just following like sheep and joining in. Fresh troops were brought in to restore order but, once inside, they too dispersed into the dark, narrow streets to join in the disorder.

The reasons why the successful stormers went beserk afterwards are very complex and it is very easy to blame the disorder on the men's desire for drink. Sitting in the comfort of our homes at the back end of

Another view of the Santa Maria (3) and Trinidad (2) bastions, taken in 1978. A road runs through the curtain wall between the bastions and through the Trinidad bastion (1) while the ravelin that once stood in front of the curtain has completely gone. The trees in front of the Trinidad bastion, and the ground adjacent to them in front of the road running through the curtain, mark the scene of the failed assaults on the breaches, one of the bloodiest episodes in the history of the British army. On the morning of 7 April 1812 this small, confined area was choked with the bodies of over 1,700 killed and wounded men of the 4th and Light Divisions who had been attempting to pass through the breaches.

Fort Pardaleras, photographed in 1914. Note how the rear of the fort has no ditch but is connected with the town by a covered way. Today the fort is unrecognisable, having been a prison and an art gallery.

the 20th century, it is very easy to condemn the men for what they did. But do we really appreciate and understand exactly what they went through? I doubt it, for Wellington's men had gone through sheer hell to get into the town, seeing their comrades slaughtered around them as they did so. These men had been pushed to the absolute limits of their endurance by the fury of their assault and this, along with the reasons stated earlier – i.e. the unfortunate reputation Badajoz had acquired as a town to be made example of, the break from rigid army discipline, plus the desire for plunder, the taste of which the capture of Ciudad Rodrigo had given them – combined to push the men over the edge. It is hardly surprising that, contrary to popular belief, not a single man was hanged, even though Wellington ordered a gallows to be erected in the Plaza Alta, for I believe that even he, the strong disciplinarian, furious at his men's behaviour, nevertheless appreciated what his men had gone through and could not bring himself to hang anybody, particularly after he saw the carnage at the breaches the day afterwards. Indeed, he wrote to Lord Liverpool, 'The storming of Badajoz affords as strong an instance of the gallantry of our troops as has ever been displayed. But I greatly hope that I shall never again be the instrument of putting them to such a test as that to which they were put last night'. It is said that some units had been promised plunder if they were successful, whilst the majority of the Allied troops knew full well that once successful, they had the right to sack and pillage the place. The French certainly knew they ran the risk of being slaughtered afterwards. What is strange is the fact that on the whole, French prisoners, unlike the town's inhabitants, were ignored. Granted, a few were killed whilst others were knocked about, but there was no wholesale slaughter and Phillipon and his staff were amongst 3,500 prisoners who were marched out of the town afterwards. It is worth noting that Phillipon could consider himself fortunate, however, for Wellington, writing a few years afterwards, wrote that, if he had put the garrison of Ciudad Rodrigo to the sword he would have saved himself the flower of his army at Badajoz. Presumably, the garrison of Badajoz, if put to the sword, may have prompted Rey to surrender at San Sebastian the following year. Wellington went on to say that the slaughtering of a garrison is not a useless effusion of blood. It is frightening to consider that Wellington's army was out of control for a full 72 hours and that all efforts to bring them back into line failed. Indeed, as Napier wrote, 'the disorder subsided, rather than was quelled'. Gradually, after exhausting themselves, the men began to drag themselves back into their camps and order was finally restored.

CIUDAD RODRIGO
AND BADAJOZ TODAY

The two old fortress towns today present a great contrast. Ciudad Rodrigo is a wonderful old town, full of narrow streets and fine architecture, whereas Badajoz has grown into a very large city, extending well beyond the limits of the walls which marked the town's boundaries back in 1812. Indeed, it is safe to say that Wellington and his men would recognise Ciudad Rodrigo with ease but would be hard pushed to find the scene of the former glories at Badajoz.

Ciudad Rodrigo still presents much the same aspect of the town stormed in January 1812, although some suburbs have since grown up around the old town. Fortunately, the old town, situated as it is on a hill, remains separate from the suburbs and is still enclosed within its old walls. In fact, it is possible to walk a complete circuit of the walls today. The main point of entry into the town is through a tunnel which, in 1812 was the site of the breach stormed by the Light Division. In 1812 a tower stood here, which quickly became the target for Wellington's gunners. It is possible to trace out the original course of the wall by following the fausse braie, which still remains today dividing the ditch into two as it did in 1812. In fact, the fortifications are in superb condition everywhere at Ciudad Rodrigo. Passing through the tunnel into the town, one should immediately look over one's right shoulder and there, up on the wall, is a brass plaque, unveiled in October 1993 to the memory of Robert Craufurd, who lies buried beneath the walls at this point. The plaque was erected by the Royal Green Jackets, the descendants of the old Light

'The Storming of Badajoz, 6 April 1812' after a painting by Atkinson. An officer of the Light Division stands at the foot of the breach while his men attempt, in vain, to pass through it.

The section of castle walls at Badajoz which was scaled by Kempt's brigade of the 3rd Division. The walls are lower here, and this almost certainly explains how the stormers were finally able to make their way up and over the walls.

Division, and the wording done by Gilles Hallam Mills, formerly of the King's Royal Rifles, whose great-grandfather, John Mills, served in the Peninsula with the Coldstream Guards.

It is possible to walk up on to the ramparts and gaze out over the glacis and down to the distant remains of the convent of San Francisco. This was the route taken by the Light Division when it stormed the breach on the night of 19 January 1812. Craufurd himself was standing on the glacis, to the left of the road as you look out from the walls, when he was mortally wounded. Once through the breach, the men of the Light Division made their way along the ramparts upon which you are standing, clearing them as far as the Great Breach, which is situated at the far end of the walls. Walking towards the Great Breach takes you past the cathedral and immediately you cannot help noticing the large chunks of stone which have been snatched out of its walls and the damage wrought to the balustrade. This is the result of both British and French artillery. The Great Breach lies at the angle of the walls at the northern point of the town and is marked by a plaque inside the ramparts. It was here that Mackinnon was killed when the great mine exploded during the assault.

Looking out from the ramparts it is easy to see how the Greater Teson dominated the town. You can still see the Teson from the walls of the town although some somewhat ugly blocks of flats have been built during the last twenty or thirty years on the site of the Lesser Teson. It is certainly worth walking up on to the Greater Teson if you can manage to negotiate the numerous wire fences and the railway. Getting to the top affords you a British gunners' eye-view of the town. Sadly, it is not possible to obtain the same view that Jac Weller managed to get for the photograph in his *Wellington in the Peninsula*. Weller visited the

A view of the castle enclosure or alcazabar. It was along this section of the walls that Picton's 3rd Division made its attack by scaling the walls with ladders. The point marked (4) is where the Spaniards themselves placed a plaque to mark the spot where the walls were scaled, although ladders were placed all the way along the walls to its right. (1) and (3) are old gates, while (2) is merely a tower. Some time since 1812 the gardens that can be seen at bottom left were dug out, although the original level of the ground here can still be determined by the grass-line along the foot of the walls.

ABOVE **It was from this tower, now a military hospital, that the French flag flew throughout the siege of Badajoz. Lieutenant Macpherson of the 45th Foot climbed the tower once he had got into the castle enclosure and promptly hauled the flag down. Not having a British flag to hand, he took off his red jacket and ran that up instead, an event marked by the Sherwood Foresters on each anniversary of the storming.**

battlefields in the late 1950s and early 1960s and his photographs provide a good barometer as to just how much some of the battlefields have changed. You will also find two forts on the Greater Teson that were built by the Allies during the summer and autumn of 1812. Wellington knew that the Teson was the town's weak point and was determined not to let the French have the hill as easily as he had won it. The forts, which are still in fairly good condition, are mentioned briefly by Jones and in the diary of John Mills, who came across them being built when he was returning to Lisbon in November 1812.

Returning to the town, a walk to the main plaza is recommended in order to give visitors an idea of what it was like immediately after the storming, the successful stormers spilling out into the plaza and setting fire to the odd building or two and generally making a nuisance of themselves before order was restored. Continuing on through the town you finally arrive at the old Moorish castle, now a luxury hotel, which is where Governor Barrié surrendered. From the castle it is easy to see the route taken by O'Toole's Portuguese as they stormed the Roman bridge over the Agueda before setting to work dealing with the two French guns situated in what is now the hotel's garden.

Badajoz, on the other hand, is a desperately disappointing place to visit, although it is a place I have certainly grown used to in the fifteen years I have been visiting it. Situated on the banks of the river Guadiana, it lies on the very busy route to Lisbon and thus is far more industrialised than Ciudad Rodrigo. When is a castle not a castle? Well, you will discover this if you visit the Moorish alcazabar, situated high on the hill at the north-east angle of the town. You quickly see that the famous castle of Badajoz is not a castle at all, merely an enclosure within which Phillipon hoped to make his final stand. Situated within the enclosure is a military hospital, on top of which is a tower. It was from this tower that the French flag flew during the siege and is where Lieutenant Macpherson of the 45th ran up his own red jacket after hauling the flag down. You then have to walk to the walls themselves, for it was along this stretch of the walls that the men of the 3rd Division placed their ladders

to escalade them. There are a couple of plaques outside on the walls, one of which is said to mark the spot where Picton's men went up. It is further down towards the area of the breaches and is situated at a spot much lower than the walls at the castle enclosure. Perhaps this explains why the 3rd Division were finally able to get up on to the ramparts.

It is very satisfying to walk from outside the castle walls to the area of the breaches. In doing so, you are walking down the hill towards the Rivellas, the rivulet which was dammed at Fort San Roque. Today, the course of the Rivellas is marked by a concrete waterway. The San Roque fort still stands, although it appears to be home to a sort of second-hand car dealer. This, sadly, is typical of Badajoz. When I first visited the town in 1983 I didn't expect to see scaling ladders still standing in the ditches and battle debris scattered about. Then again, I didn't expect to see washing lines strung out across the ditches at the San Roque and Tête du Pont. Life goes on.

Large sections of the mighty walls have long since been demolished but, fortunately, the area of the three great breaches remains intact. The ditches have gone, of course, as have the ravelins, but the walls remain and, in fact, the site of the breaches in the Trinidad and Santa Maria bastions are marked with the dates '1812' picked out in holes which once held cannon balls. The balls have disappeared but the numbers are clearly visible. It is an eerie feeling to touch the walls within which so many hundreds of brave men lie interred. A road runs through what was once the curtain wall between the two bastions. It is worth pausing to reflect upon the fact that this busy, scruffy-looking road marks the site of one of the bloodiest fights in the history of the British army.

It is difficult to follow the route taken by the 4th and Light Divisions on the night of 6 April 1812 owing to the large suburb which now covers the

LEFT 'Wellington visits the scene at the breaches on the morning after the storming of Badajoz'. This painting by Caton Woodville shows quite graphically some of the means used by the French to block up the breaches. The savage chevaux-de-frises can clearly be seen, bristling with sharp sword blades. Wellington actually wept when he saw the shattered remains of his storming columns in the breaches. He is known to have wept openly on only two other occasions, the first being at the funeral of Edward Charles Cocks, at Burgos in 1812, and the second after the battle of Waterloo in June 1815.

BELOW, LEFT Wellington rides into Badajoz after the storming to find his men enjoying the fruits of their success. He was not pleased by the events which followed the storming and which lasted for a full 72 hours, although he knew what a hellish experience he had put them through. Certainly, no soldiers were executed, contrary to popular belief.

ABOVE, RIGHT The castle walls today. It may give readers some idea of the height of these walls to note that the author (centre) plus his two accomplices (Ensigns Gedge and Skinner) each stand about six feet tall. Given that a ditch had been dug at the foot of the walls to raise the height even further, the achievement of Picton's 3rd Division becomes all the more remarkable.

RIGHT Another depiction of the assault on the breaches at San Sebastian. After a painting by Wollen.

ground. However, it is possible to find the site of Fort Picurina, part of which still stands defiantly in the grounds of a small playing area. From here it is an easy and satisfying task to pick out the buildings on the skyline, buildings which feature so prominently in contemporary paintings. Fort Pardaleras has changed and was, until recently, a sort of art gallery, having earlier been a prison. Again, it stands in the middle of a very scruffy residential area.

On the northern bank of the river Guadiana, high above the water, stands Fort San Christobal, the site of the attacks in June 1811 and the place where Phillipon and his staff surrendered on the morning of 7 April 1812. The fort is still in good condition, if a little scruffy inside. The walls are superbly protected by the glacis and it is easy to see why the attacks in 1811 failed so miserably. Returning to the town takes you across the Roman bridge with its numerous arches. At the town end of the bridge stands the gate of Las Palmas, with the Tête du Pont still intact at the other end. Once you have crossed the bridge into the town, a right turn takes you to the San Vincente bastion, escaladed by Leith's 5th Division.

The town itself is not a very pretty picture. The cathedral remains much the same, as do some of the smaller streets around its base. But it is not easy to imagine the shocking aftermath here when Wellington's men went berserk for 72 hours, sacking the place until they had no energy left to continue. It is far easier to imagine the dreadful scenes by returning to the castle, for it was here, through a gate which is still possible to find – today it is simply an archway – that the wild, battle-maddened soldiers of the 3rd Division first broke into the town to begin their orgy of destruction. To the right upon leaving the gate is the convent whose nuns were abused and raped, whilst to the left of the gate is the Plaza Alta. It was here that many of the men gathered and was the location of the gallows which Wellington had erected. The streets in this area of Badajoz are still small and narrow and here it certainly is possible to imagine the events which followed the storming. Tragically, it was not to be the last time that Badajoz experienced such traumas, for, when the town was captured by Franco's forces during the Spanish Civil War, many of the defenders were rounded up and executed in the old bull-ring, whilst the town itself was badly treated, particularly by Franco's Moroccan troops.

WARGAMING THE BADAJOZ CAMPAIGN

INTRODUCTION

In *Tristram Shandy*, by Lawrence Sterne, will be found a vivid description of how the narrator's Uncle Toby, assisted by the faithful Corporal Trim, dug up a bowling green to re-create extensive fortifications and siege lines in miniature and removed lead weights from sash windows to obtain the raw material for model artillery pieces. Few readers of this volume will have the opportunity to emulate them – though many might wish otherwise! – so below are suggested more practicable and economical methods for besieging the 'Keys to Spain' as wargames.

CAMPAIGN/SIEGE KRIEGSSPIEL

Methods for plotting strategic and grand tactical manoeuvres on maps and resolving any engagements that may result therefrom according to the principles of the original military training game, the Prussian Kriegsspiel, have been described at some length in other titles in the Campaign Series (see, for example, the Wargaming Appendices to *Salamanca 1812* and *Vittoria 1813*, also by Ian Fletcher) and need not be repeated here. To re-create this campaign, however, it will be necessary for the Umpire – essential in any 'closed' wargame – to add some further rules to portray the two sieges themselves, whilst remaining true to the underlying structure.

   In addition to maps of the theatre of operations, the opposing players, portraying General Barrié, General Phillipon, Colonel Lamare and their staffs, or Wellington, Fletcher and their staff officers, will require plans of the two fortresses and their immediate surroundings

The site of the breach in the Santa Maria bastion, Badajoz. The year '1812' was once picked out in cannonballs and, although the balls have long since been removed, the holes and the figures are still discernible at the top.

upon which to mark their troop deployments. The plans should not be completely identical: the French players' plan must show all fortifications in detail, including the calibres, positions and arcs of fire of the various guns, and will depict any alterations or repairs to the works made since previous sieges; that of the British players must portray only Wellington's intelligence of both fortresses prior to the sieges.

If the Umpire does not wish to force the British players to follow the historical siege plans descibed in this book, he may stage a preliminary roleplay, in which the players taking the roles of Wellington, Fletcher and Burgoyne debate the possible points of attack, to arrive at the plan that will be followed in the subsequent game. A detailed understanding of early 19th-century siegecraft will be essential for those playing the engineers.

The Umpire must have an accurate, objective map, covered with transparent plastic, upon which he can sketch the parallels, saps and batteries that the besieging troops attempt to construct, with a water-soluble marker pen. By careful measurement of angles and ranges on this map he will be able to determine whether any of the fortress guns can enfilade the enemy's saps, or bring an overwhelming volume of fire down upon a battery under construction; calculate the distance gained or works completed, and inform the player commanding the besiegers of the casualties suffered by the working parties that day. Similarly, at the appropriate times, the Umpire will determine the effectiveness of counter-battery and breaching fire, resolve sorties by the garrison and decide the success or otherwise of attempts to storm outworks.

To determine the time required to execute each stage in the progress of a siege, the Umpire should devise 'norms' based on information in this book, Ian Fletcher's previous work on this campaign and Jones's Sieges &c., vary them in proportion to the odds favouring each side, and apply a random factor in the form of a die roll. Such a game could be played with separate teams in different rooms, in an afternoon. Alternatively, the Umpire would have time to create more detail in his reports to the opposing players if the game were played in real time, by reporting the outcome of each daily turn by telephone or e-mail each evening.

Any of the games described below to re-create particular aspects of the sieges in greater detail could be introduced by the Umpire at an appropriate moment to provide greater atmosphere for the players.

A SIEGE MATRIX GAME

For a shorter, more sociable – albeit less realistic – 'fun' game of one, or both, sieges the Umpire might care to adopt the Matrix Game structure, devised by Chris Engle of the USA, first published in his Experimental Games Group newsletter, EGG, and since featured in *The Nugget*, the journal of Wargame Developments.

Before the game commences, all players receive a general briefing describing the strategic situation, containing intelligence known to all commanders in the area, and a list of key words to aid the composition of Arguments, which should include all technical terms used in siegecraft, together with any explanations necessary for those who have not already read this book. The game is 'open', each turn representing a day, but players may have secret personal objectives and individual

The Roman bridge over the Guadiana at Badajoz. It was across this bridge that Phillipon galloped with his staff to make good their escape to Fort San Christobal after the fall of the town. Phillipon crossed the bridge from right to left.

maps or plans on which is marked information known only to the characters they portray. Then the players, in the same roles suggested above, and the Umpire take their places around a map of the theatre of operations and a plan of the besieged town, which should be covered with self-adhesive transparent plastic to permit the drawing of parallels, saps and batteries erected by the besiegers, and their erasure if destroyed by a sortie, using water-soluble marker pens. Troops and other resources may be represented by symbolic bases of 6mm models, or by cardboard counters.

Each player, in an order determined either by the Umpire to reflect the current situation, or randomly by a die roll, then has to present an Argument, comprising an Action, the desired Result of it, and three Reasons why it should succeed. The Umpire listens to all the participants, in order to discover whether any player is declaring a Counter-Argument to one that has been made already that turn, in which case he must determine the respective strengths of the opposing propositions, or have the players concerned dice to resolve the contradiction, and to decide the order in which the success or otherwise of each Argument should determined. He must also classify each Argument as either Weak, succeeding for a score of 5 or 6, or only for 6 if judged extremely weak, on a normal die; Good, succeeding for 4, 5 or 6; or Strong, succeeding for 3, 4, 5 or 6, or even for 2, 3, 4, 5 or 6 if very strong. The players then dice, in turn, and the map or town plan is updated accordingly to show the situation at the end of that day.

For example:
Player A (portraying Sir Richard Fletcher):
'The besiegers commence digging saps forward from the second parallel (Action), and succeed in advancing fifty yards today (Result), because their morale is high after the capture of Ciudad Rodrigo (Reason 1), the weather is fine so the soil is dry and easy to excavate (Reason 2), and there is no effective fire from the fortress as a consequence of our successful counter-battery fire over the previous three days (Reason 3).'

Player B (portraying General Phillipon):
'The garrison makes a sortie against the heads of the saps being dug from the second parallel (Action), which prevents the besiegers sapping forward more than a few yards (Result), because the sortie is timed to coincide with the change of troops in the trenches, which are left unguarded until the next working parties enter them (Reason 1), the attackers [putting down an appropriate number of troop markers] considerably outnumber the trench guards (Reason 2), and the fine weather made the English think a sortie without cover of darkness or rain was so improbable that they were taken by surprise (Reason 3).'

Umpire:
'Both arguments accept that the weather is fine and that the besiegers will commence sapping forward today, so those aspects of the situation are not in dispute. General Phillipon has made a Strong Argument, so he will throw first, and the sortie will succeed for 3, 4, or 5, preventing the digging of ten yards multiplied by the die score, and if a 6 is thrown, the damage to the parallel and the loss of vital tools will also prevent any sapping tomorrow. Should it fail, however, the troops will suffer a minimum of 20 per cent casualties, and 40 per cent if only a 1 is scored.

'If the sortie fails, then the besiegers may sap forward some distance after repulsing the enemy for 4, 5 or 6, the distance gained being 5 yards multiplied by the die score. Lower scores will indicate the disruption to the working parties was such that the rest of the day was occupied in evacuating wounded, repairing damage to the parallel and the sap-head, constructing more gabions and bringing up new tools.'

Whilst some wargamers have complained that a Matrix Game is neither a matrix (a fair comment!), nor a game, its 'open', face-to-face structure does not seem inappropriate to the sieges described in this book, which were conducted according to a long-established set of principles, so that the besieged could predict the next stage of the process with some degree of certainty, and take suitable counter-measures.

GAMES OF VARIOUS ASPECTS OF SIEGE

Both wargames described above attempt to re-create the perspectives of army commanders and their staffs and of the governors or commandants of the fortresses. The following low-level 'skirmish' games or roleplays are intended to provide players with a more vivid portrayal of the grim reality of sieges for individual officers and men than that afforded by the highly symbolic representation of the campaign game, into which they may be incorporated, at appropriate moments, should the Umpire and participants so wish. A series of such games, covering each different stage of a siege from digging saps to storming a breach or attempting an escalade, could focus upon the experiences of a company or battalion of British troops. Every player should be allocated several individual characters, of various ranks, so that there is a good chance that he will have at least one surviving personality in the final assault.

'NAVVY'S WORK': SAPPING

To illustrate the hazards of digging zig-zag trenches towards a fortress, the Umpire will lay out a section of the first or second parallel, using tape or some of the model siegeworks which may be purchased from various manufacturers of wargame scenery and accessories, in the same scale as that of the 15mm or 25mm figures portraying the working party on a 1:1 man:figure ratio. Players will move their own personal figures of British officers and men, and non-played characters will respond to the former's orders, but the Umpire will control the fortress artillery, and attempt to hit the head of the sap by relaying the guns and adjusting their elevation, using a dice-based deviation system, such as that to be found in Rohne's *Artillery Kriegsspiel*, translated by Bill Leeson, and the random shots of sharpshooters. He must devise some rules to determine casualties amongst the players' characters – largely a matter of chance! – damage to gabions and tools, and the forward progress of the head of the sap.

'THE WORKMEN MASSACRED ... THE WORKS MATERIALLY DAMAGED': SORTIES

In this scenario troops from the garrison attempt to break into the siege lines, to destroy trenches and batteries, and to delay the progress of the siege by carrying off vital tools. Can the relief trench guards counter-attack in time?

Sorties can be fought using the figures and scenery suggested for the previous game, using 'skirmish' wargame rules such as *Flintlock & Ramrod*, those in Paddy Griffith's *Napoleonic Wargaming for Fun*, or Donald Featherstone's *Skirmish Wargaming*, with the addition of rules devised by the Umpire for the destruction of trenches, gabions and tools, or a set invented by the participants themselves.

'DESPERATE BAYONETING': STORMING OF OUTWORKS

Attempts to storm outworks such as Fort Picurina, besides adding colour to the campaign Kriegsspiel, make challenging one-off tactical games as an alternative to the typical wargame encounter battle in open countryside, even if one does not wish to re-create an entire siege. A model of the work could be carved from expanded polystyrene or upholstery foam, built by laying a cardboard 'skin' over 'ribs' scaled up from the profiles and cross-sections in Jones's Sieges &c., or constructed from all the Lego bricks that participants can temporarily borrow from their offspring!

A simpler, but less visually pleasing, alternative would be a two-dimensional representation, either a large-scale, coloured plan as a playing board, or outlines of the glacis, ditch, parapet and rampart marked out on a large floor with coloured tape or chalk. Ideally, the man:figure ratio for such a game should be 1:1, so that the model work can conform completely to the figure scale, but should that prove impossible then a small man:figure ratio and an aesthetically pleasing compromise between ground and figure scale must suffice.

'PASSPORTS INTO ETERNITY': THE BREACHES

Players take the roles of officers and sergeants commanding the Forlorn Hopes and storming parties and the Royal Engineer officers responsible for leading them to the breaches under cover of darkness. Before the game commences, the latter are permitted a brief perusal of a sketch map of the fortress, upon which are marked the breaches, and must thereafter rely upon memory and clues given by the Umpire to guide the storming parties, by calling instructions to the commanders of the

When the 3rd Division finally broke out from the castle enclosure and into the town itself, many of them turned to their right and immediately fell upon this convent. The nuns inside were raped and abused by the victorious British troops who, driven to the point of madness by the fury of their assault, literally went berserk. Tradition has it that the regiment involved in the incident was ordered by an outraged Wellington to wear its regimental badge upon its fly-buttons.

troops, who move backwards on hands and knees across a large floor, moving their model soldiers as they go.

A tape grid laid out before the game by the Umpire, linked to a similar grid superimposed over his master plan of the fortress, enables him to tell the players what they can see immediately around them, from which they must deduce the route to the breach. Upon the Umpire's plan will also be marked the chevaux-de-frises, mines and other obstacles placed by the French before the attack, to be revealed to the players when appropriate.

Die rolls, or chance cards can determine exactly when the storming parties are detected by the garrison, whereupon the French player can decide when to open fire and detonate the mines. Thereafter, the British players must simply endeavour to storm the breaches, lead their men forward, rally confused and disordered men in the ditches and try to stay alive.

'HUZZA, THERE IS ONE OVER, FOLLOW HIM!': THE ESCALADE

The problem is to re-create the hazardous business of climbing a ladder and gaining the rampart whilst under fire and gaining the rampart, when model soldiers cannot easily be placed upon miniature ladders, nor be moved up them. A possible solution is to create a boardgame-style display for each ladder raised successfully, based upon that old family favourite Snakes and Ladders. Each ladder, shown in foreshortened form as if from above, is surrounded at its base by squares where troops awaiting their turn to mount are placed, and overlaid by a grid, corresponding to the number and position of the rungs and the base size of the figures or counters being used. Several squares on each ladder, selected at random – their number and position varying slightly from one ladder to another – are marked as 'hazards'. Special dice numbered 1, 1, 1, 2, 2, 3 determine how many rungs each figure climbs, always starting with the topmost. Any figure landing upon a hazard square is deemed to have been hit and falls, usually suffering death or such a grievous wound that he will not mount the ladder again. A saving throw of double 6 on two ordinary dice could represent those close shaves and lucky ration biscuits/watches/lockets/Bibles that turn a bullet to give players' own characters a slightly higher chance of surviving!

A figure who falls may also cause the one immediately behind to fall – dice to see. Figures pressing up behind with higher die scores than obtained by a figure may push him forward one rung.

Once a figure reaches the parapet, he will have to defeat a French soldier in single combat, using a version of the traditional game Paper, Scissors, Stone, to gain a foothold on the rampart that will enable further soldiers to climb safely. A ladder can be pushed over if sufficient French soldiers gather around its top to outweigh the troops upon it. A falling ladder is assumed to kill all upon it, except the players' own personal characters, who may dice for a lucky escape, and should be replaced by another ladder, with a different combination of hazard squares, when raised again. Such a system would enable the players to attempt to re-create the daring exploits of Lieutenant James MacPherson of the 45th.

A symbolic version, in which one ladder represented all those raised, could be used to portray the escalade of the castle, whilst another display showed the breaches, to give an overview of the whole storming.

'THE TOWN'S OUR OWN – HURRAH!': AFTERMATH

Since both the sieges described in this book are notorious for the collapse of discipline that followed the storm, it may not be inappropriate to offer some suggestions for gaming the plundering of Ciudad Rodrigo and Badajoz, as a fitting conclusion to a series of games portraying the individual experiences of typical officers and men. Players whose personal characters have escaped death or mutilation in earlier games now have to keep their honour and survive the sacking of the town.

The game will take place on a model of a Spanish street, to the same scale as the figures, with buildings whose removable roofs reveal detailed interiors, like those in the popular Western Gunfight participation games to be seen at many wargame shows. Spanish civilians, parties of French prisoners and gangs of marauding British soldiers will be controlled by the Umpires, using preprogrammed actions, chance cards or dice to determine their movements and reactions.

Each player will have a 15mm or 25mm figure, representing each of his surviving officer or sergeant personal characters, together with an individual personal briefing for each one. These briefings will assume that the players' characters are men of honour, who will refrain from joining in the plunder and rapine, for this game is not intended to celebrate indiscipline and depravity. British officers must attempt, albeit at the risk of their own lives, to rally and regain control over disordered, drunken and rioting troops, to protect French prisoners and helpless Spanish civilians – and, occasionally, to rescue beautiful Spanish girls from the licentious soldiery …

A GLOSSARY OF SIEGE TERMS

Bastion These were strongholds which, when linked together, formed an enclosure around a city or town.

Breach An opening made in the wall or rampart of a fortified place.

Chevaux-de-frise Formed of large pieces of wood stuck full of spikes, sword blades or long nails. These were used to block up breaches and to prevent entry by enemy troops.

Curtain The curtain is simply a wall that joins together two bastions.

Ditch The ditch is a hollow channel made beyond the rampart and goes all the way around the place. The edges of the ditch are made sloping with the slope nearest the place called the scarp and the slope nearest the besiegers called the counterscarp.

Embrasures Openings made in fortifications through which guns or muskets are fired.

Fascines Composed of bundles of branches like faggots, six feet long and tied in two places. Used to strengthen or replace walls of trenches or other places.

Gabions A kind of basket, about three feet high and usually of the same diameter, filled with earth and used to provide cover during sieges.

Glacis The sloping ground immediately before the ditch, over which attacking forces would pass before descending into it.

Gorge The part of the work next to the body of the place where there is no rampart or parapet.

Lunette A work placed on both sides of a ravelin to defend it, or simply a small fort, eg the Picurina and the San Roque.

Palisades Strong wooden stakes about nine feet long driven into the ground, usually in the covered way, about a yard from the parapet of the glacis.

Parallel A place of arms. Deep trenches in which the troops who are working on the approaches to a fortified place can be supported. Normally about three parallels are dug.

Parapet A parapet is a bank of earth raised upon the outer edge of the rampart. Used to protect the besieged and to give cover to defenders to enable them to fire down into the ditch.

Rampart A masonry wall or a great bank of earth around a town to secure and defend it.

Ravelin A work placed in front of a curtain wall and used to cover the flanks of a bastion.

Saps Saps are trenches made and carried on under cover of gabions, fascines, etc., and are pushed forward from the main parallel to establish batteries and other parallels.

The Puerta Capitel, Badajoz. It was through this gate that the 3rd Division finally passed from the castle enclosure into the town. The French had blocked it after the castle fell, and fired upon any man who tried to pass it. Nevertheless, the 3rd Division eventually succeeded in breaking out, which was the cue for the sacking of Badajoz to begin.

INDEX

(References to illustrations are shown in **bold**. Plates are prefixed pl. with caption locators in brackets.)